EFFECTIVE

HUNTER-KILLER
OPERATIONS

INTEGRATED TACTICAL WARFARE SERIES VOL. 2

R.J. GODLEWSKI

Eliminating elitism from defense.

TABLE OF CONTENTS

DEDICATION

To absolute freedom from tyranny.

In veneration of Saint Michael, the warrior archangel who singlehandedly cleansed Paradise from evil and fights for every soul destined to be with God. May I do for the earth what you have done for Heaven...

ACKNOWLEDGMENTS

To God the Father, the Son, and the Holy Spirit, without Whom I would find no talent, no opportunity, and no friends with which to affect either my trade or my interests.

Deo gratias.

CHAPTER ONE:
LETHALITY IN WARFARE.

WRITING DURING THE early 19th century, Prussian tactician Carl von Clausewitz implied that kindness in battle represented the worst mistake that military personnel could commit, for not to prosecute war with the maximum use of military force represented a grave fallacy. For Clausewitz, since war was such a deadly business, these mistakes were despicable. It was a thought that, a few decades later, American general William Tecumseh Sherman would characterize within his famous statement that war was, beyond anything else, absolute hell.

During this modern era, military practitioners have often deflated the concept of *all out war* for more subdued efforts designed to win the "hearts and minds" of 21st century inhabitants of this planet; people whose concept of warfare remains more akin to tribalism than nationalism, more insurgency than confrontation. The inherent problem with this approach is that humans have become increasingly accustomed to perennial conflict during the past fifty years than had during the five decades prior to that.

The more people become familiar with war and strife, the less likely they are offended by threats of martial involvement. That is, humans necessarily adapt to the status quo and often do not shift in his or her opinion even if greater stress is forced upon them. This serves at work, at school, in matters of health and education, and, of course, in war. In fact, the argument rests; there have been relatively few 'long duration' wars from the period 1812 to 1953, attesting to the belief that wars of recent history are painfully long for indigenous populations. *However*, wars have always been tormenting in length – even those of comparatively brief duration – merely that the industrial age has convinced some that a new technology here or a new perspective there will always shorten the latest "war to end all wars"

Arguably, the longest of wars remain those that are not declared as such, including the Korean Conflict, Vietnam, the Cold War, the "war against drugs", and so forth. These stagnant conflicts morph into the human subconscious and, more often than not, slide away from the collective mind. As with the case of the younger, MTV generation – who largely ignored the September 11th, 2001 attacks in New York City and Washington, D.C. by the first anniversary[1] – the wars that lose the front page of the news cycle become politically non-existent. It is these "non-existent" wars, unfortunately, that fester equally non-existent peace.

The lesson here, of course, is that war is *war* and not peace. There remain few rules beyond winning at all costs. Those that try to "civilize" conflict end up doing little beyond brutalizing peace and represent those "kind-hearted people" that Clausewitz warned about. Individuals that, for whatever ill-conceived intent, led to such atrocities as Cambodia, Darfur, Rwanda, Bosnia, and every other genocide frequented by humankind.

How, then, should humans wage war should they fail on every account to avoid it? Are they to launch massive, battalion-centric conflicts that the West prefers to keep the Military Industrial Complex rolling in profits? Alternatively, should they retain the conscript-heavy insurgencies that less

---

[1] Mark A. Cwiek, "America after 9/11" in eds. Gerald R. Ledlow, James A. Johnson, and Walter J. Jones, *Community Preparedness and Response to Terrorism: Volume 1: The Terrorist Threat and Community Response* (Westport, CT: Praeger, 2005), 14.

developed nations prefer simply to confuse and confront the rest of the planet? Unfortunately, both approaches represent attrition-style wars that serve little but to force one side or the other to call it quits through the lack of personnel, materiel, or public support. In the end, the underlying problems for the conflict continue to simmer on until another group takes up the challenge – usually to even lesser avail.

Sharpening the sword.

Effective military operations require both intensity of action and singularity of purpose. There can be no hesitation, no limitation. They add organization to human martial affairs and ensure that the highest levels of ethical standards are conceived of and implemented. For these reasons, no activity ever undertaken as a pure military function should serve to broaden the sufferings of innocent persons or damage civilian structures purposelessly. Unfortunately, Western-style militaries remain both destructive and indiscriminate.

Even today's widespread use of unmanned aerial vehicles (UAVs – erroneously referred to as "drones"), which purport to represent surgical strikes, often involve significant collateral damage. The use of UAVs to target far-flung adversaries merely extends the emotional distance between those targeting the individual and those giving the order (or performing the function) to kill. Because of this, such standoff attacks make them easier to utilize.

Military force should *never* be used simply because it remains easy or emotionally distant; combat operations should always be used as a last resort and to protect human value – whether national or spiritual – exclusively. In this regard, we can apply the concepts of 'just war' as outlined by the *Catechism of the Catholic Church*:[2]

1. "the damage inflicted by the aggressor on the nation or community of nations must be lasting, grave, and certain;

2. "all other means of putting an end to it must have been shown to be impractical or ineffective;

3. "there must be serious prospects of success;

4. "the use of arms must not produce evils and disorders graver than the evil to be eliminated. The power of modern means of destruction weighs very heavily in evaluating this condition."

While these conditions remain to govern war between nations, we can extrapolate from these, guidelines for waging battles *within* such wars:

The conditions for justified force

No military operation should be undertaken unless an aggressor has irreparably harmed the nation under which those military functions remain governed, to which the declaration of war (or the declaration of war against it) remains the only viable option. In this regard, combat operations cannot be isolated from war nor used as a political tool. Without the support of its national constituency, any military force simply becomes the brandishing arm of the executive, leading to tyranny itself.

Military operations must be reserved for those missions where diplomatic, legal, and social efforts have failed or have proven to be ineffective. As a component of war, martial operations must involve a

---

[2] United States Catholic Conference, Inc., *Catechism of the Catholic Church* (New York: Doubleday, 1994), Paragraph # 2309.

conscious effort on the part of the national governance for imposing "actionable justice" against the party of aggression. That is, military action must be taken exclusively to "render the aggressor unable to inflict harm" – not merely deflect its intentions.[3]

Military forces must not be committed into battle unless there remain extraordinary prospects for success of the mission undertaken. Disasters occur when military or political leaders establish combat operations with severe restrictions imposed upon any particular unit. As there is no legitimacy in going to war without justice, there is no justice in placing military personnel at risk without sound doctrine for unit defense and mission success.

Military operations must only employ those weapons and personnel directly required to achieve its mission. Here is where "surgical warfare" comes into existence. One does not carpet-bomb to target an enemy leader anymore than they use a sledgehammer to drive in a tack. For weaponry to remain effective, it must adhere to three basic laws of ethics: the weapon must only target individuals that remain active combat troops; weapons must retain a 'trigger person' whose responsibility for the kill rests entirely within his or her hands; and the weapon cannot leave any destructive remains that require cleanup. In this regard, the most effective military weapon remains the individual firearm.

These conditions require that any effective martial operation be placed as close to the enemy as possible. Furthermore, these military operations must consist of *human* functions, for technology simply expands the cultural, emotional, and physical distances for the act of killing, which

---

[3] Ibid., #2266.

merely dilutes the justice inherent within authentic combat operations.

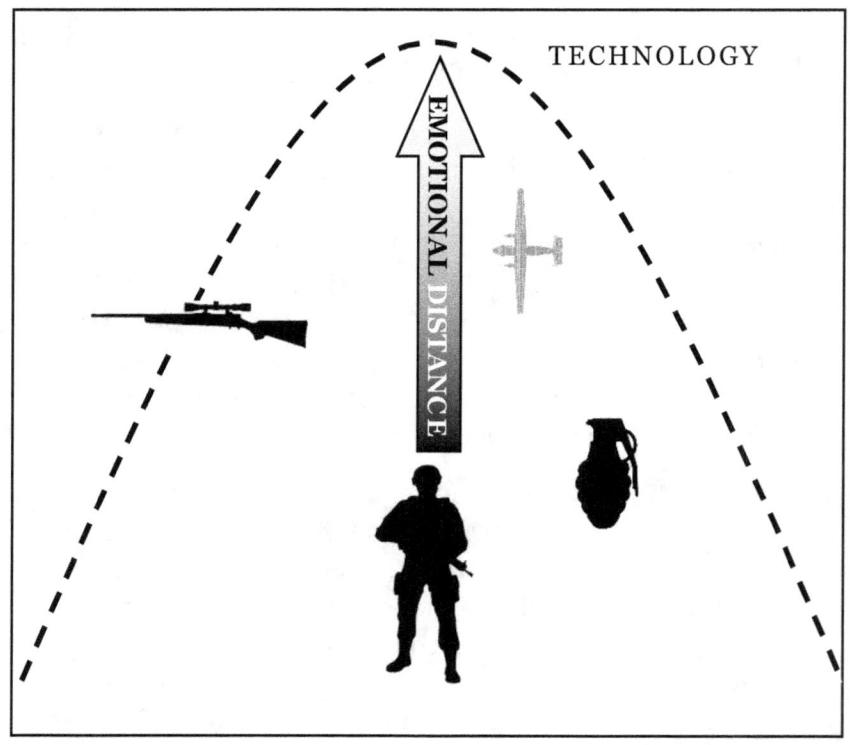

Figure 1. Comparative distances to target.

Figure 1 reflects these distances, as grenades, sniper rifles, and aircraft simply remove the defender from the physical and psychological presence of killing an aggressor. In the case of a sniper rifle, for instance, the shooter observes merely an optical generation of the target, much as how one views a subject through a television screen. A grenade, for its role, removes the user from psychological culpability for an attack. That is, once thrown; the soldier simply turns away and permits the explosive device to kill whomever resides within its lethal range. Use of aircraft merely extends this reach on several orders of magnitude as the distance between attacker and target extends over several thousand feet and, perhaps, miles.

These examples show how military and political leadership can become immune to the brutalities of war and *appreciation* adds value to any consideration. If one does not truly appreciate the actions that he or she undertakes, they remain likely to regenerate these actions without proper consideration. This escalates into indiscriminate warfare, turning military forces into little more than terroristic groups.

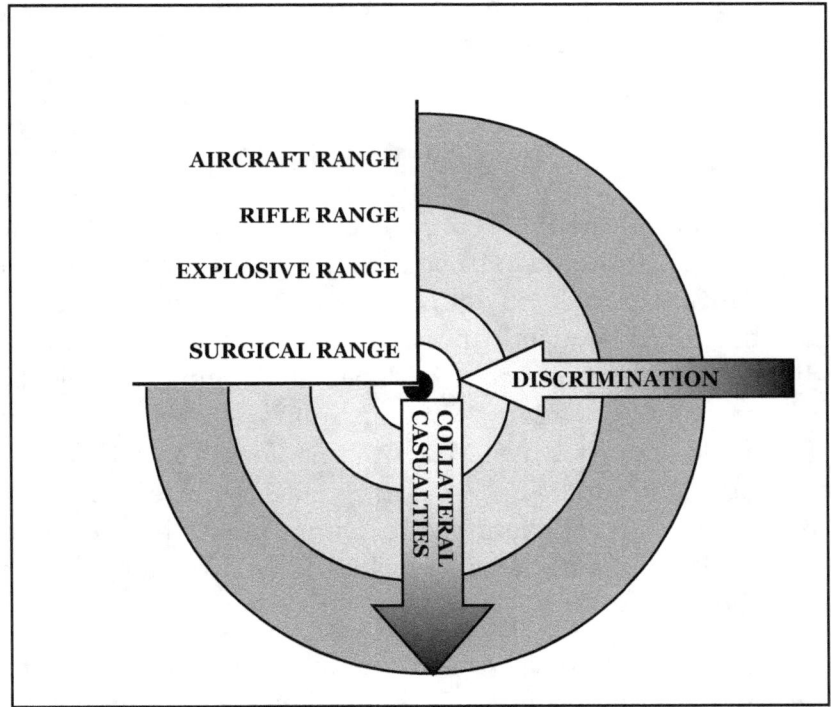

Figure 2. Relationship between weapon range and collateral damage.

Indiscriminate warfare remains ineffective, leading to additional casualties and greater resources required to fight the present conflict (see Figure 2). To counter this trend, effective military operations must continue to select those targets that offer *force-multiplication* – individuals whose incapacitation offers great damage to adversarial forces – and attack *only* those targets with weapons that offer the most lethality *and* controllability. In other words, military forces comprised of highly disciplined, trained, and capable individuals operating with the least exposure to the environment and centralized command.

Justifiable force requires the offensive military operation to single out aggressors from any surrounding population and to dispatch them with the least force available. This requires the active element to *physically* locate and actionably *identify* the culprit so that the target may be neutralized with absolute certainty.

Thrusting the sword.

Once the commitment to employ lethal force is reached, the military organization must begin to lay plans for effective use of that lethal group. No longer can these military forces – today, becoming focused upon special operators to the point of diluting the very concept of "special" – remain subject to transient political leaders. Nor can military forces exist with the equivalence of tenure. Yes, military forces must function according to national leaders' will, yet they must be formed with a true sense of dignity and commitment to excellence. Here is where most of the world's militaries fail and fail miserably.

Within any group, there remains the prospect for one or two individuals to taint the reputation of that organization through malice of intent. Many professionals classify these individuals as "pirates" and left unchecked, they will easily persuade the actions of other, less malicious individuals through incite or pressure. Even the most prestigious of organizations are not immune from this – recent examples including major league sports franchises, U.S. Navy SEAL units, and even the Roman Catholic Church. Where excellence is sought, there are others willing to diminish it for personal glory, ambition, or notoriety.

To reduce exposure to such pirates, military units must remain small enough to develop personal camaraderie and yet large enough to function as holistic groups. In other words, small enough so that each participant holds influence upon all others and yet large enough that should the particular unit in question suffer extraordinary casualties, the unit can be "retired" from frontline service.

This last element requires some discussion; as traditional thinking holds that casualties are replaced as soon as possible with fresh troops. In fact, this diminishes the effectiveness of the entire unit as time and effort spent equating the new individuals with their veteran comrades draws away from unit preparedness. In this regard, military units should be viewed as "families" – once casualties are realized, the military unit in question transfers to other responsibilities based exclusively upon its remaining potential.

Where countering arguments prevail, one only needs to clarify that smaller units allows for *more* units. That is, if one particular unit is 'retired' due to casualties, another readily exists to take over pending obligations. Henceforth, all military divisions should be managed – and organized – from the ground upwards rather than the bureaucratic status quo of creating massive entities that may or may not concern themselves with the sharper end of martial conflict.

The fundamental role of *any* military unit remains to impart lethal influence upon an adversary. This practice is achieved through four primary methods:

1. *Direct killing of adversarial individuals*. This has been the role of martial conflict since Cain and Abel. Briefly stated, this remains the principal accounting of warfare – to kill as many enemy soldiers as is possible within the timeframe permitted while keeping your own forces intact. The side that emerges with the most killers available wins – generally. The problem with

this facet of lethal influence is that, beyond intended targets, the aggressor usually finds itself alienating third party institutions, most notably nation-states not currently involved within the conflict;

2. *Destruction of enemy assets.* Even when direct killing is not productive, parties involved within the conflict generally aim to destroy as many enemy assets as possible to sway both political leadership and constituent populations that to fight against you remains decidedly costly. Here is where the carpet-bombing raids conducted during the Second World War received their notoriety. True, the Allies, for one, did not wish to kill all those civilians but *someone* had to pay for Axis aggression. Of course, the Allies were targeting specific military and industrial facilities so civilian casualties were largely ignored in these 'round the clock' airstrikes that did little but to turn Europe and Japan into vast wastelands;

3. *Posturing.* This psychological tactic simply employs military forces as a deterrent against attack wherein larger and more wealthy nations parade their militaries in front of the news media while lessor groups take to the streets to promote their own 'Cause' as the main reason for existence. Posturing usually serves those who cannot fight (due to inadequate resources) or will not fight (due to popular opinion). Generally, military units hate posturing for it forces them to train without martial release. However it is employed, posturing serves to feign military strength in order to influence adversaries without the host group resorting to actual combat;

4. *Intimidation.* Although it may incorporate any of the three elements above, intimidation rests as the primary reason for the existence of military forces in the first place. The safest method for organizational security to exist – security representing the absence of

uncertainty – remains to terrify adversarial forces into believing that they will suffer extraordinary consequences if they attack. Where this element diverts from simple posturing is through *reputation*. That is, intimidation does not function well if the intimidator does not bear sufficient experience in carrying out its threats. In this regard, street gangs the world over influence a great many because they are known to destroy, maim, and murder at the drop of a hat. No one questions their desire to carry out threats and this is precisely the reason why nations develop special operations military assets: to intimidate adversaries into believing that "our side" bears the baddest group on the planet.

Each of these four missions bear numerous subsets, but no matter how political and military leaders seek to spread influence throughout the broader world, they cannot escape adherence to one or more of these primal factors. For instance, killing adversaries remains far more effective if you can intimidate them into running away. Similarly, it remains easier to posturize if you possess the capability of wiping out entire cities *en masse.*

Unfortunately, for either of these elements to work, one needs to employ them productively and herein is where most of the world's militaries fail. They simply set internal standards of engagement that serve little beyond confusion at best and hamstringing military forces at worst. No matter how easy it remains to 'draw lines in the sand', once those lines have been crossed, the gloves need to come off.

What remains lacking today, sadly, is that most military forces – including those serving powerful nations such as the United Kingdom and the United States – fail to possess tenacity, patience, and resolve. Only Israel, and this seems to be subdued as of recent, bears a reputation for going after its enemies for long after grievances have been affected. It is as if a broad "statue of limitations" exists within republican democracies that allows enemies to escape if they can remain alive for a certain period of time.

In the grand scheme of global, martial politics, the placing of individuals upon any kind of 'hit list' should immediately distinguish that individual as eventually terminated. That this is not widely practiced says more about political futures than it does about military substance. Yesterday's allies become today's enemies and vice versa. If little else, this reality serves to dilute the concept of war itself; if someone is worth killing ten years ago, then they should remain worth killing today. Conversely, if someone bears merit in becoming an ally – at any point – then why would *anyone* seek to destroy that individual?

When one thrusts a sword, it remains very difficult to retrieve that weapon until it has met its target. A bullet in flight, similarly, bears little option but to reach its target. When military forces are deployed, they *must* carry out their intended – *not* political – mission, for to recall them "in flight" risks future implementations of the four referenced elements above. Here is where the primal aspects of hunting and killing come into focus – and need to be addressed anew.

Summary

War remains the most lethal of human endeavors, a collection of hostilities designed to force one side's will upon another. To wage it effectively, the victor must resort to the sharp end of the spear and kill as many "key personnel" as possible from the ranks of the enemy. Unfortunately, many combatants taint mission objectives by not addressing the discipline necessary to wage effective war. Rather, misguided soldiers resort to expectations of attrition warfare, which remains detrimental to even the largest nation.

CHAPTER TWO:
ENGAGING THE HUNTER.

MAN REMAINS A primitive creature, despite modern society's best intended efforts to evolve humans into some form of technology-centric, socialized global citizen. At their basic level, an individual will resort to any manner of deceit, violence, or thievery to achieve whatever objective rests within their mind. And it matters little as to that person's sex, ethnicity, nationality, religion, or economic status; people are simply hard-wired for conflict without restraint.

We know from Dr. Stanley Milgram's Yale University studies conducted during the 1960s that sixty-five (65%) of the human population can be led into inflicting deadly force upon an innocent individual with very little prompting – no more than an "authoritative figure" bearing a while lab coat and clipboard – and with modern social media and instant data communications, this potential "prompting" has magnified exponentially.

In a sense, we are surrounded by a sea of threats and the only way to survive, sometimes, remains to terminate those threats immediately. Or as "immediately" as we are prepared to accept. In this regard, the world, indeed, rests populated by wolves, sheep, and sheep dogs – though the latter remain exceedingly rare and underused (mostly as 'pets' rather than servants).

Nearly every person becomes infatuated with technology, for we all desire to make our lives more convenient, more productive for the least effort required. For outdoorsmen, this could mean the latest in trail cameras, improved archery, and natural-print camouflage. Unfortunately, as with their military brethren, modern hunters, gamekeepers, and even photographers remain weighed down with complicated gadgetry that serves little purpose but to bulk up their presence at the cost of efficiency in the field.

It should, therefore, come as little surprise that the best hunters in history have been those relatively undressed natives of America and Africa. When human migration turned towards the colder climates of Europe and Northern America, the addition of heavier clothing simply introduced the inconvenience of carrying one's body-habitat along with them. This may very well explain the present fascination with lugging as many "conveniences" along as possible to forestall our psychological reluctance to return to our primal roots.

As civilization fully emerges into the first techno-social century, we have come to depend upon wireless telephones to communicate our messages (almost always in text format), Global Positioning Satellites, or GPS, to navigate our automobiles, and even tiny household gadgets that can answer every question that we may fancy a need for. Our beverage cans now contain, in large print, how many calories they impart upon our bodies and our trips to the grocery store suggest when, precisely, our meats and vegetables were delivered to that particular location. Gone is the need to remain self-sufficient, for *everything* we need to survive and thrive is laid out upon our fingertips.

Nevertheless, in all the known universe, humans represent the only creatures with both a physical body and a spiritual soul comprised of an independent will. What this means, for the uninitiated, is that humans can freely adapt their presence within the physical world through no other incentive than "it is there". That is, *only humans* could freely venture out of Equatorial East Africa to find themselves hunkering down in Eurasian caves to wait out the latest blizzard. Animals migrate by way of necessity, but humans can also sense that the "grass is greener on the other side of the fence", even if that appreciation is based upon false data.

To experiment within these new homes, humans had to not only fabricate shelter against unknown climates, they had to forage for unknown plants and hunt for unknown animals. They, in a sense, migrated away from being exclusively gatherers into becoming both hunters and farmers. These two disciplines paved the way for humans to survive within the subsequent millennia – and no human could survive very long today without either meat or produce.

These attributes remain so ingrained into the human intellect, that modern people have all but forgotten them – save for at the dinner table. Herein is where individuals recognize certain palates and desires. Nevertheless, these buried characteristics remain exclusive to humans from amongst the animal kingdom and must be recovered to produce effective hunters (as opposed to the 'weekend warrior' types restricted to legislatively dictated seasons).

The successful *permanent* hunter retains the following capabilities:

- ✓ **Terrain appreciation.** Perhaps the most recognized and yet neglected trait of the successful hunter remains terrain recognition and appreciation. This irony develops from an observation that, yes, hunters must understand the environment of their quarry but fail when that hunter resorts to technology or provisional status to reflect upon that particular environment. In other words, the hunter is likely to know the forest and the general wildlife, but fail to appreciate the peculiarities of individual trees, winds, ground, and other aspects of the forest. A *true* hunter misses little, observes all, and recognizes importance within the obscure. They understand wind patterns from the shape of the trees, flooding patterns from the texture of the ground, and migration patterns from the lay of the hills and valleys.

✓ **Development of the senses**. Here is where an individual dispenses with the expected to extract information from the obscure. He hears when most others prefer to see, smells when most others prefer to touch, and judges when most others prefer to estimate. Even the presence of thousands of conflicting odors, sounds, and vibrations do not go unnoticed. Imagine if our senses were akin to a ball of Velcro®, our daily lives would be covered with the multitude of "debris" clinging to our mind, each bearing a unique 'fingerprint' of what happened before our arrival on scene. This allows us to predict what may come next. The reason, of course, that we bear *five* senses instead of one comes from the need for both redundancy and confirmation. Our eyes and ears, for instance, can both be used to detect the direction of fleeing game; eyes can determine movement and our ears, the doppler effect.

✓ **Creativity**. Hunting remains an art, despite that most of its technology hails from science. Tracking prey involves an intuitive understanding of one's environment, how best to employ that environment for tactical advantage, and, most of all, the cunning to defeat the prey's own primal self-preservation mechanisms. This ability swirls within creative thought and the astute hunter must remain far more than someone "toting a gun for the kill" (or even a camera for that matter). To be successful, one needs to defeat "Murphy's Law" on several matters and no one has yet devised a surefire scheme to confront the unimaginable.

✓ **Persistence and resilience**. The single most reason that the clear majority of hunters fail rests with giving up on the hunt. In the recreational arena, this has more to do with legislative periods and domestic responsibilities than anything else, but when the 'prey' can destroy the hunter at will, 'surrendering' remains tantamount to extinction. In the modern era with, say, personal time off (PTO) allocations in the workplace, people have become accustomed to employing sick days for everything from the sniffles to golf outings. As a result, very few – if any – individuals are pushed to his or her limits of endurance. One could not, for instance, consider walking five miles one way in a suit and tie, operating a tractor-trailer rig with severe food poisoning, or riding a motorcycle in 10° F. temperatures just to make it to work on time or otherwise complete a required assignment.[4] Nevertheless, these represent basic human achievements, and such discloses our ability to endure inconveniences when so required.

✓ ***The killer instinct***. Unless one were after a photograph, the basic premise of hunting remains to kill the prey. Herein represents the secondary reason why most hunters fail: humans retain a modern tendency to refrain from taking lives – even of animals. We will discuss this issue more in depth within subsequent chapters, but the inability to take down prey remains averse to most modernized individuals accustomed to shopping at the local market for his or her dinner and snacks. That said, almost every person on the planet bears the ability to kill, though most of our capabilities dispense through the relatively common act of "losing one's temper". When pushed beyond a certain point, almost everyone will turn to martial behavior to defend their life or

---

[4] Memorandum for the record, experiences of the author, R.J. Godlewski.

that of a beloved comrade. To hunt is to kill and to do otherwise simply turns the act into a mere 'sport'.

Having briefly discussed these personal characteristics, we can now turn our attention to their employment in greater detail, dispensing with the 'civilized' approach to rather neglected subjects in order to fashion a more reasonable appreciation from the student.

Terrain Appreciation and Awareness.

Our environment involves a four-dimensional world that requires astute multi-tasking to understand and appreciate. To traverse this world of ours *without disclosing our presence* is not an easy task to do, despite the assurances of Hollywood and action/adventure novelists. One is not normally expected, for instance, to possess the ability to sneak upon a whitetail deer and whack its hind quarters without the animal fleeing beforehand, but any decent hunter *should* possess this ability.

Terrain appreciation enlists four distinct features encompassing the geographical, biological, climatological, and historical aspects of the environment. That is, at any given moment, a hunter may have to understand the flow of water through valleys and ravines, the presence of particular flora, the direction from which prevailing winds flow, and recall upon past experiences (personal or otherwise) to gauge an effective solution to any present problem. These attributes cannot be isolated from one another, nor will they always appear within calculated amounts.

The hunter must absorb his environment rather than merely trespass upon it and this involves a great deal of counter-prey efforts too: to proceed effectively through any environment requires one to keep from being noticed by others, be they animal or human in nature. Unfortunately, modern efforts usually trend towards carrying an unreasonable burden upon one's person, such as 80-pound packs, personal armor, Kevlar® helmets and the like. These do little beyond isolate the hunter from the environment and offer up many opportunities for 'prey' to become aware of the presence of the hunter instead.

Because of these problems, the most effective training towards terrain and environmental appreciation involves dispensing with nearly everything carried *into* that particular environment, such as artificial equipment, clothing, and odors. *Anything* foreign to the location will signify an interloper and this, beyond anything else, can turn the hunter into the hunted. And when the intent of hunting remains to kill or capture, being on the receptive end places the individual into unnecessary harm.

To progress through an environment successfully, literally requires an individual to place their body into the unique position of representing an eternal sensor; that of turning one's body into a mechanism for the detection of the slightest vibration, temperature variation, and movement. That is, without conscious consideration, one must feel for the presence of obstacles, changes within the climate, and, most importantly, detect the presence of threats. This is where becoming an "information sponge" comes into play; to survive requires one to be more knowledgeable than anyone or anything else he or she is liable to encounter.

If we view *any* environment as alien, then this requirement is met without fail. In other words, if we dispense with commonality, we forfeit any change for routine or expectation. We observe this, on albeit a very minor scale, whenever we consider our reactions within our own homes as compared to, say, visiting a friend or relative's. In the former case, we never lose sleep over the sounds of a house settling, the hot water heater starting, or the myriad of other sounds that our subconscious minds tend to sift out as commonplace. In the latter, our minds are fresh and often wake us to unusual sounds that the owner's own minds have long since ignored. Expectation can lead to subversion and compromise – the two deadliest vices in survival.

Each type of terrain heralds a different perspective, one fostering such a change in perception:

* *Open.* Open terrain represents that environment where trees and elevations do not necessarily restrict one's view. Here, only an individual's eyesight and the weather prevent them from observing far afield. The relative openness of this terrain requires careful attention to the sounds, odors, and silhouettes presented by the hunter.

* *Mountain.* Mountainous terrain, for the sake of this discussion, represents that environment where hills and mountains abruptly alter the terrain, forcing individuals to consider its effects on vision and climate. Elevations also create problems for travel, camping, and tracking prey. More attention is thus focused upon personal survival and safety than towards the actions of the prey. This dilutes the ability to follow other, more intellectual, targets.

* *Desert.* Desert terrain combines elements of both open and mountainous environments, depending upon the precise location of the hunter. Expanding upon the aforementioned attributes, deserts offer complex climatological changes and magnify, as but one sense, sound. Heat during the day and relative cold during the night play havoc with inexperienced hunters and offer a range of conflicting sounds and sights to behold.

* *Jungle.* Jungles, unlike most other environments likely

to be encountered, offer their own entire ecosystem of life and subcultures. Isolated from the rest of the world, life within the jungle abruptly challenges intruders. The density of vegetation, heat, humidity, and boundless threats conspire to reduce the effectiveness of *all* individuals traveling through that particular environment. Even native travelers find comfort in transiting *known* paths and frequenting trusted locations. To accept this convenience, however, may prove fatal to the hunter for he or she may be duped into convention.

* *Arctic.* Like the desert, Arctic terrain can consist of both hilly and open environments, with the added challenge of extreme cold to confront the hunter. Many of the useful features of other locations – such as the ability to dig into the ground or partake of flowing water – are not as readily available. The hunter, knowing this, must make allowances for carrying additional supplies to compensate for the lack of food, shelter, and clothing. Similarly, any attempts to cook, warm oneself, or even trap prey telegraph that individual's location to others.

* *Urban.* An urban terrain is not a common environment to consider when the discussion rests upon hunting, but it *does* represent an environment likely to be encountered nevertheless. In this regard, "urban" means any centralization of artificial structures and dwellings. Whether one is considering a few thatch huts or sprawling metroplexes, urban environments offer profound challenges to the hunter. First and foremost is that *all* human environments involve artificial planning and development. What this means is that, say, residents do not follow the same natural laws as would occupants of a desert or jungle. That is, compare Mexico City with Lake Tahoe, for instance. Or Los Angeles and Ansager, Denmark. Just because

humans congregate does *not* mean that they follow
expected architecture anymore than they can be
expected to confirm to predictable behavior.

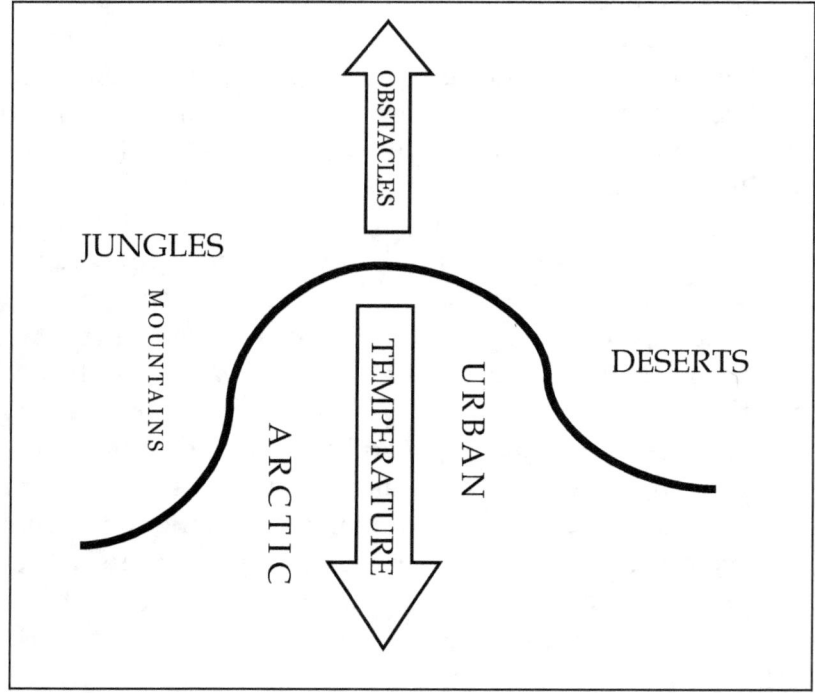

Figure 3. Representative features of various terrains.

To transgress any terrain requires the individual to
develop a 360° Sphere of Awareness surrounding their
person. This means that nothing escapes his or her
attention – no sound, no perception, no thought.
Everything within that individual's environment must be
detected, assimilated, and mentally filed away for
strategic advantage. This is not an easy task, as most
individuals fail miserably in development of the senses.

Sensory Development.

There remains little to escape the human senses. Left unobstructed and healthy, the ears hear every sound that enters them, the eyes behold every sight they witness, and the nose filters every odor it inhales. Only the human mind elects to ignore or not, largely through the conscious soul empowering that mind. Unfortunately, the hunter cannot ignore *anything* that has not been first analyzed, categorized, and itemized. He or she must forego the subconscious desire to equate novelty with threat and force such considerations to the fore of conscious appreciation.

Without proper conditioning, however, an abundance of information may overlord human senses, translating required data into "background noises" that may confuse and irritate the uninitiated. For instance, traveling within the northern woods of America, a hiker may not appreciate the shrill 'rachet' call of a Redwing Blackbird, the technical 'security alarm' sound of the Cardinal, the melodic scales of the Baltimore Oriole, or especially the chaotic whistling of the Starling. These calls, all intended to communicate with the animal kingdom, pass off as static to the untrained human ear.

Nevertheless, these *sounds* alert other humans too. The well-disciplined mind and cultivated ear can detect thousands of sounds and understand intimately their meaning. Such an individual can ascertain whether intrusion, for instance, is from a fox or a human. Birds make different sounds based upon differences within the perceived threat. And this merely points out one aspect of operational aware; humans bear five senses.

Touch represents another key sense often ignored by ill-trained hikers and holiday vacationers – as but two disinterested groups. Touch imparts a wealth of knowledge from the presence of moss upon trees, the direction of prevailing winds, even the breath of a nearby animal during the darkest of nights. With the exception of, perhaps, taste, touch remains the only *active* sensorial response of an individual. That is, a conscious effort can be made to determine *what* is being felt whereas sight and hearing merely require observation

Consider an individual walking down a trail following a night of massive storms. His sight can behold the damage of trees by visiting fallen branches. His nose can smell the dampness of the leaves and trunks. Yet, upon coming across the footprint of a deer within the mud, he can reach down and *touch* the ground to determine just how dry that spot is and, therefore, decide *when* that track was made. Eyesight found the track, smell formulated a situation, but simple touch determined *time.*

Because humans naturally tend to employ the wrong senses – or, perhaps, just the weakest ones – at any given time, the astute tracker, gamekeeper, soldier, conservationist, photographer, etc. needs to condition him or herself to avoid using the 'natural choice' when considering these senses. To avoid this problem, the following measures can be undertaken:

   ✓ *Conduct training in virgin territory so that past exercises do not suggest repetitive responses.* Humans bear a talent for ignoring things experienced within a very short time, so to prevent this the student must relinquish *any* opportunity for bias (in the form of expectation) during drills by continuously granting them the 'shock' of new terrain, new climates, new locations, etc.

   ✓ *Restrict all senses not involved within the training.* Simply put, if you are conditioning the ears, then you would want to diminish 'noise' generated from eyes and skin. The student should sit within the woods, for instance, blindfolded and make notes of what he or she hears (yes, people can write while blind) and then, afterwards, compare his or her notes with what their eyes finally reveal. This can be done within the relative safety of the home as well. Any time that permits an individual to "remove" one of their senses should be employed to develop the others.

✓ *Combine classroom knowledge with field experience.* Here, we find a difficult challenge for we must properly infuse theoretical knowledge in with practical exercises – *without* compromising the integrity of the activity. For example, train students with the various *expected* calls of birds within a given training location and then ask field teams to not only identify the animals but listen to see if they can discover precisely *when* the birds detected the presence of the students through changes in pitch or frequency.

✓ *Employ cognitive exercises.* Many household goods truck drivers are trained with puzzles (many akin to the videogame Tetris®) to aid them with loading trailers against prejudicial considerations such as setting sofas on their sides while stacking washer and dryer in-between the arms. Written puzzles such as |r|e|a|d|i|n|g| (translated as "reading between the lines") or **GNINNUR** (translated as "running backwards") provide a fun way of getting students to consider alternatives to every perceivable indicator. The same holds true, say, with notetaking; people tend to write notes in the same manner as they read, which in the West endears them to placing prominence on things written on the top left of the page and ignoring things at the bottom. Instead, notes should be written in cryptic symbols known only to the student, differing fonts, unusual colors, positions on the paper, etc. to force him or her to stop and think about what they mean less he or she dismisses pertinent information subconsciously.

Cultivating the proper use of senses both supports and rests upon the next key element to discuss.

Cultivating Creativity

Within its briefest definition, creation represents the production of a thought or idea from within the mind of the creator and then manifesting that product into tangible form for others to consider. For instance, Michelangelo always "saw" David within that large block of marble, but until he chiseled away the excess most people only saw a coffin-shaped rock. The same holds true with Beethoven's Fifth Symphony; he knew the arrangement well before he finalized the notes for musicians to consider. Simply put, creation is taking that which could not have been perceived beforehand and turning it into reality.

In warfare, creative technique shepherds in a range of options that, when properly executed, confound an adversary. For instance:

- During many historical naval battles, ships were disguised as anything but military ships to goad the prey into assuming benevolence or weakness.

- During WWII, the British sent a brave pilot to drop a helium-filled soccer ball covered with luminescent paint on a vaunted Nazi airbase to "decoy" the Germans into believing that such a ridiculous stunt had to have involved some form of super-secret weapon. Even when, after two weeks of research, German scientists pronounced the ruse, Nazi leadership still insisted on solving the device.

- With the advent of smokeless powders, military snipers began to wear Ghillie suits and employ natural vegetation as camouflage to conceal their presence from enemy soldiers and observers.

Despite these examples, however, *creativity* is a purely natural function amongst the animal kingdom. Animals from butterflies to buffalo employ creative deception to hunt and to hide. It remains humans, although, that build creativity into its most innovative levels.

Hunters engage within all manners of creative thought, ranging from choosing the best camouflage to hide from targeted prey on through using doe urine to attract bucks. Nevertheless, it rests with the hunting of *predators* that, perhaps, creative tactics come into play the most. Here is where the hunter will likely mimic the cries of a wounded cottontail rabbit or yellow-shafted flicker to attract coyotes. Understanding the gluttonous nature of these canines, trained hunters can deceive the animals into expecting an easy dinner.

In martial environments – whether hunting for dinner, survival, or influence – creative action simply serves as a force multiplier for strategic advantage. At a minimum, creativity serves to keep the user attuned to changes within his or her environment. By that, we mean, that the creative individual usually avoids stoical or traditional behavior. A creative personality sees solutions rather than questions, challenges rather than obstacles. He or she takes what is *available* and fashions a tool or a procedure out of that asset to affect a chance in outcome of any situation.

For instance, if an artist were faced with replicating the image of a criminal, they may use either pencil, crayon, or oil paint to produce the representation. Conversely, a writer may employ a computer, a cell phone, or a simple pad of paper to jot down the notes for a future novel. Creativity remains a function that employs whatever tools are available to the artist.

To cultivate this approach amongst the less-creative can be quite harrowing, particularly if the instructor is working with purely analytical personalities who see specifics rather than pastels. These individuals do not observe anything fluid or interpretable; *everything* must be quantified or qualified. They see not "a hotter than hell" day, but one that remains precisely "100.5 degrees Fahrenheit". Nevertheless, even these finite individuals can be taught to see the infinite; the forest for the trees.

Part of the solution rests with breaking down problems to their core. This is not done to overly quantify the issue; rather, such actions may serve to force the individual to observe that one large problem may consist of several smaller problems, thereby suggesting that what was once viewed as, say, "5", now remains "1+1+1+1+1". It *still* remains "Five", mind you, but the problem presented has been expanded so that the individual no longer sees merely the earlier digit – or challenge.

Much the same can be done with digital photographs that, contextually remain the same, but whose colors have been altered for effect. Now, the individual's mind must reconsider information it had previously deciphered. With this approach, we may institute a "problem". For instance, *what color* has been altered and, given a choice, *which color* would [the student] replace the missing hue with in order to bring back the original image if the missing color no longer be amongst the options?

Another exercise involves a group of individuals whose backgrounds have been briefly provided to the student with the task of affixing these limited biographies upon the proper subject simply by watching their mannerisms, talk amongst themselves, and even choice of clothing or other habits. These exercises allow for the predominately analytical nature of the student while fostering the recognition that certain things must be deposited creatively into reports that remain lacking within quantitative data.

As we are attempting to foster a sense of hunting within our personnel, further training exercises must involve the naturally changing world of the great outdoors. That is, all personalities – including analytical minds – bear the primal traits of survival, competition, and innovation within the recesses of their subconsciousness. To stimulate growth, one must approach problems outside the sterile classroom environment. Expectation remains the one aspect of humanity that squashes independent thought. In the modern, civilized world, this reality simply diffuses into broader entitlements. This is why the younger (as well as a few older) generation remains fascinated with videogames; it does not take a great leap of the imagination when virtual worlds recreate nearly every fathomable environment from farming on through historical battles and into the mind-numbing considerations of intergalactic warfare.

Creativity can best be cultivated simply through *denial* of solutions within expected problems. For instance, a person taught how to manage a classroom of kindergarteners, can now be introduced to training puppies. Instead of getting a room full of five-year-olds to finger-paint the paper instead of the walls, they now must get several mixed-breed canines to "wait" for meals or toys. The effect remains the same; the student must consider alternatives outside his or her expectations. Similarly, a student may be presented with the challenge of writing a narrative about a rather mundane subject. Now, however, the student is presented with the requirement to edit the narrative but with *selected words removed from their permissible vocabulary*. This action slowly dilutes the student's preference for certain words and forces him or her to creatively describe the scene with *new* words thrown in to shatter their preferences.

Remember, the basis for all creative work entails the production of "something" out of nothing so that all others will understand what had heretofore existed solely within the mind of the artist. Anyone can, for example, adequately describe what he or she ate for breakfast. Yet, if the person remains a talkative soul, they may have difficulty writing down their thoughts on the matter. Similarly, if the person is not vision-centric, he or she may have problems in replicating the colors associated with, say, their Denver omelet or the texture of their French toast. Creativity *forces* them to communicate beyond their comfort zone, think beyond their consciousness. Or, simply, to spring a trap for a species they may have never encountered beforehand but must consume to survive.

Persisting at Tasks

If there is one aspect of hunting that determines success or failure, it would arguably represent *persisting* at the assigned task. In this regard, resilience can best be defined as commitment to success beyond all costs or efforts. In hunting, for instance, the hunter either kills his game or he or she returns home empty handed; there is no purpose in restating tales of the "big one that got away". In the game of survival, starvation rests as its own accelerant.

Unfortunately, a vast portion of the human population merely seeks to shoulder the minimum effort for the job required. Consider the office environment, for example. A typical salaried shift may be, say, from 7 A.M. to 4 P.M. with an hour lunch thrown in at 11 A.M. to keep workers happy and content. Nevertheless, a great many workers do not *start* at 7 A.M. nor do they leave precisely at 4 P.M. On the contrary, he or she may finally reach their office, after stopping off at the water cooler or coffee pot, around 7:20 A.M. and be waiting for the elevator door to open at the end of the day at 3:40 P.M. Nor do our lunches begin at 11 A.M., not when we must visit the restroom at 10:50 A.M. or end an hour late when our best friend (at least at work) regales us with tales of their latest golf outing.

Specifically speaking, most people – especially Westerners – remain rather unproductive, which leaves us as "weekend hunters" at best. Far be it for an individual to spend three days walking into a premier hunting ground or suffering another four days dragging his or her trophy prey out from the bush. People, now even within the deepest reaches of Africa or South America, are convenience driven. We do what we *want* to do, not what we *must* do. After all, why hunt for venison when dinner can be had at the local grocery for a fixed cost and all our calories can be displayed for convenience. Do we not stand in line for a whole five minutes for the effort?

Such discussions remain popular amongst the human population, but these thoughts can be deadly within a harsh environment where survival knows neither time clock nor checklist. Individuals who have survived stranding within mines or adrift at sea are properly called "heroes" for they persisted beyond the reasonable limits of human expectation. They proved that the human mind, as much as it is, remains little more than a reducing value when compared with the human spirit that can conquer even towering mountains.

This ability for resolve, for persistence at task until completion, remains a vital element for hunting, whether with gun or camera. In this regard, we can eliminate all discussion involving amateurs – those hunters or photographers who merely undertake the effort for joy or pastime. *True* hunters and photographers – those whose livelihood rests upon catching their prey in gunsight or viewfinder – do not cease until he or she completes the goals for which they set themselves out to achieve. For the hunter, this may mean bagging that priceless mountain goat or simply bringing home enough whitetail venison to shore a depleted refrigerator. For the photographer, the "perfect" picture may result from days' of planning for the correct sun angle or exposure to create one of those lifetime poses that end up within the pages of a coffee table almanac of local species.

Stalking prey, as with the broader discipline of tracking, requires the hunter to remain both proficient with technology and adept at primal tactics of camouflage, silent movement, and deadly persistence. One breach of either trait and the target would flee or attack. And since people remain the outcasts within *most* environments, he or she is likely to remain at a disadvantage when confronting any prey – let alone, say, another individual hellbent on killing the tracker instead.

To adequately blend into an environment requires an individual to make slow, methodical motions that absorb oneself into whatever vegetation exists. This, in turn, will reduce the anxiety of whatever animal life lives within the surrounding area. Finally, little disruption amongst both the flora and fauna of the area and less likely will there be detection from other humans. This capability founds itself upon patience and persistence, twin attributes of any successful hunter.

Persistence, patience, confidence, and knowledge create a linear equation for hunting, and these attributes must be developed concurrently if they are to supplement one another. For instance, if an individual bears little confidence or knowledge of his or her environment (not to mention task at hand), then it remains probable that they will not cultivate enough patience to be persistent in his or her goal. Conversely, someone with a great deal of knowledge and, likely, overconfidence in their capabilities may overreact and spoil opportunities through his or her own lack of patience. Here, persistence may lead them into the wrong path or assume the wrong target.

Accordingly, simply remaining persistent within any task does not necessarily produce good; a hunter or outdoorsman *must* retain focus and singularity of purpose, the latter representing a breakdown of large goals into smaller, easily managed ones fostering motion and direction. We can visualize this by, again, employing the tactics of an outdoor photographer (the field retaining all the qualities of hunting with the decidedly greater need for both creativity and technical knowledge).

In our scenario, the photographer's interests lay with the capturing of a whitetail deer on camera for a series of magazine articles or books:

- ✓ The photographer has chosen to focus upon whitetail deer because this animal remains fairly common within almost every location throughout the United States and, therefore, almost every reader of the publication will recognize the animal with little added discussion.

- ✓ Next, the photographer notes various locations where trees line a riparian environment that fronts numerous cornfields. Here, the targeted deer find both refuge in the trees and a steady diet of corn to consume.

- ✓ Knowing that whitetail deer are rather nocturnal in nature, the photographer sets up a schedule where they will be in the woods during days where the sky is clear at sunset and the wind remains relatively calm to avoid carrying the photographer's scent to the animals.

✓ Reconnoitering the area for days, the photographer observes two trails leading in from the river that are likely used by wildlife coming into an opening (*two* trails provide the animals with the security of an escape route should one be blocked by a threat).

✓ Finally, the photographer positions him or herself against the thicket, back to the sun, and *patiently* waits for deer to arrive once the sun sets, taking advantage of the "golden hour" – the hour before sunrise or following sunset when contrast from shadows makes photographs present greater depth.

The five steps enumerated above illustrate how even the rather innocuous task of photographing wildlife requires a profound persistence through easily identified tasks. One does not simply rush out to the woods and take pictures of deer; all animals are finicky and even remaining motionless towards a curious doe, for example, will bring about a series of loud snorts from the animal warning all others that an intruder remains on the loose.

More precarious rests the prey that can turn into a predator himself without warning. Here is where the tracking hunter must remain one step beyond his or her prey for spooked deer simply run away. Persistence, therefore, remains far more than simple endurance or resilience. It requires a great deal of planning, absorption of knowledge, and martial instincts. The hunter endures because they are, more than anything else, a *killer*. Whether for food, clothing, shelter, or tools, the *act* of hunting rests with personal survival. Failure to bring home the venison, skins, and bones meant demise for early settlers and nomads alike.

The Name of the Game: Killing

Militaries, contrary to modern socialistic interpretation, are *not* humanitarian or peacekeeping organizations. They are, more than anything else, institutions designed to force national will upon others – even if this merely means defending one's territory. The side with the most *lethal* forces wins. That our present fascination with industrial accounting leading to attritional campaigns as a preference does not change the foundational equation of history: enemies kill their enemies.

Here is where martial science meets with martial art; both creative personalities and their more stoical analytical brethren bear roles within the killing of one's adversaries. Pragmaticism defines a need for liquidation and innovation offers a bountiful harvest of options to carry out that task. Whether one bears a flintlock musket or a B-2 stealth bomber laden with bunker buster nuclear bombs, the inherent desire to dispatch the adversary, *permanently*, remains the same.

Volumes have been written on the need for – and implications of – teaching otherwise "civilized" recruits to kill when so required. The advent of action-adventure movies and virtual reality computer games have done much to desensitize a gullible population but, as with the case of the latter, all our efforts seem to produce little more than "couch commandoes" who prefer to conduct all their vices via the conveniences of the cyber world.

A similar problem rests with the domestic hunting population itself. Our techno-centric society rests upon feeding deer off-season, modern camouflage patterns, compound bows, and readymade tree stands from which to await our prey. Killing, therefore, simply becomes an extension of all that technology – permitting the "hunter" to escape his or her culpability through endless distances of physical and emotional artificialities. Even highly regulated – or not – official executions involve hoods, lethal injection apparatuses, or multiple shooters (only a few of which bearing live ammunition) to shield parties away from what is otherwise the taking of another person's life.

To kill, sometimes even repeatedly, requires those individuals involved to eliminate *all* artificial barriers from this act of killing. The hunter is effectively ceasing the life of another animal, silencing its soul (all living things bear souls; humans simply possess one that is both eternal and external to his or her body). When a hunter kills a deer, for instance, it terminates that animal's ability to function within its environment, with the implications of it fostering interactions with other living things within that particular environment.

Think about this for a moment. Suppose a factory worker died from an accident, an illness, or simply natural causes. In the grand scheme of things, the company would either hire another worker to fill that individual's place or charge existing employees to add additional tasks to his or her duties. In either case, a *conscious* decision was made to deal with the loss of the former worker. This is not how the natural world behaves.

The killing of a deer, for example, does *not* immediately lead to other deer filling in raising fawns, distributing food stocks, or adjusting their natural behavior. A dead deer is just *that*, a dead deer whose soul had been permanently silenced for the effect of the hunt. In this capacity, the hunter has removed a piece – however seemingly inconsequential – of a larger jigsaw puzzle without subsequent considerations of what his or her actions may represent. This remains the *essence* of hunting wild game, whether pheasant, deer, antelope, or wildebeests.

For comparative analysis, let us discuss the widescale shooting of American Bison during the middle to late nineteenth century. Largely done to keep the Native American population from eating, these animals were killed *en masse* depleting an otherwise massive population of beasts that, sometimes, would delay trains for days during their migration. Herein, we cannot argue that these animals were dispatched via simple killing for such actions amounted to a wholesale slaughter of another species. In the truest sense, the reduction of the bison herds shepherded in "industrial hunting" for the sake of eliminating an important (for Native Americans, primarily) source of food.

With these distinctions in mind, we can formulate a response that *hunting* is killing whereas killing is not necessarily hunting. More to the point, we can argue that hunting remains a *deliberate* and conscientious effort, further delineating the activity from less ethical considerations of random or indiscriminate killing. From another perspective, we can analogize the discussion with the concept of two adversarial soldiers employing bladed weapons – the first bearing a dagger whereas the second handles a broadsword.

Each individual will approach his opponent based upon his skill with the weapon and, most especially, the tactics he developed while learning to use that weapon. In our confrontation, the dagger-wielding solder will make quick strikes against his opponent, seeking to thrust his weapon into the other's most vulnerable organs while retreating as quickly as possible to deny his enemy a chance to counter the strike. Conversely, the swordsman will likely engage his opponent with broad sweeps, propelling his weapon outwards from his body in order to gain maximum muscular force combined with the energy of accelerated mass.

In less choreographed, massive battles, we can quickly see the outcome. Conflicts involving swords tend to produce chaotic scenes where individuals are literally hacked to death. Those involving daggers or knives tend to represent battles where victory rests upon the swift discovery of an opponent's Achilles' heel. In this latter environment, the victory tends to favor the mobile rather than the insulated. In this brief discussion, we have isolated the objective hunter from the subjective killer. Or, more accurately, perhaps, the disciplined ninja from the pretentious samurai. One kills because he is paid to do so whereas the other kills for honor and prestige.

Similarly, the true *hunter* kills for the sake of food and clothing – survival – whereas the more modern, "weekend warrior" outdoorsman kills primarily for group dynamics. That is, to kill for sport, notoriety, or braggadocio. If this were not the case, then the "hunter" in question would actually engage in hunting rather than *waiting,* which is what most amateur (defined as those who undertake an activity for the sheer love of it) enthusiasts attempt when setting out to bring home a well-pointed buck.

As we have been admittedly engaged within semantics, we must further resolve to admit that we have been pushing the discussion into a narrow focus: that of separating those who kill for need away from those who kill for the sake of killing. Militaries, for instance, kill for the sake of killing whereas police officers, contrarily, kill as a direct result of perceived need. This is also why police officers are bound by more jurisdictional rules than are soldiers. Nevertheless, neither remain effective killers despite their respective rationale.

In war, ironically, there remains no excuse for killing just for the sake of killing. So-called "accounting wars", attrition wars, siege wars, etc. do little beyond aggravate human misery. On the other hand, pretentious "surgical strikes" offer opportunities to exacerbate the underlying conditions that foster conflict in the first place. That is, history remains strewn with conflicts that destroy civilizations or engender them towards further wars.

Herein is where we find the definite need for *hunters* in war; individuals handpicked, expertly trained, and dismissed from all aspects of centralized command. Small, elite, innovative teams whose sole purpose rests with the completion of *particular* tasks – namely the tracking down and killing of key enemy personnel. Units deliberate enough to serve as *true* force multipliers through their selective targeting and termination of essential enemy personnel – the very essence of justifiable killing.

From this perspective, we can forego all considerations of *ledgering* battle; dismissing how many enemies we kill in favor of observing how effective our killing truly becomes. For example, if it remains argued that the assassination of Archduke Franz Ferdinand resulted in the launching of the First World War, what would the outcome have been had his assailant, Gavrilo Princip, been killed beforehand? Such a question, naturally, rests upon a host of suppositions of the intercessor possessing actionable intelligence, forethought of intentions, and, of course, proper timing. These are not incredulous requisites, mind you, but impractical during that time and period.

The crux of the above discussion, however, rests with the implications of killing an individual versus waging attritional war across numerous borders and alliances. The countering argument that, perhaps, the "Great War" had been primed to begin regardless of progenitor only holds merit if, indeed, war had been the goal rather than the result of contemporary politics. From hindsight, it does little justice to dwell on the various scenarios shattered by reality. Archduke Ferdinand was killed, the world went to war, and his assassin died a miserable death attributed to tuberculosis. And, in the modern era, neither individual is remembered by most of the world's population.

We broach here, perhaps contemplatively, the dire need for *precision* killing of influential adversaries; the targeted elimination of those whose death just *may* avoid further "wars to end all wars". We have, thus, entered a highly controversial discussion pitting theology, politics, strategy, ethics, and plain human decency against one another for martial superiority. And, frankly, there can be no victor within this debate for the implications rest upon a fluid understanding of factors, each as transient as are our global leaders.

This said, we *can* make a determination as to *who* should be employed within these "hunter-killer" groups, *how* they should be trained, and, even, *when* they should be employed. Within reason, of course. As with all martial considerations, the rules remain set by the victors and few others. What was permissible, say, for Pope Julius II during 1503-1513 would be inconceivable for Pope Francis today in 2018. In fact, the very concept of a 'warrior Pope' defending national sovereignty remains ludicrous for those ignorant of both history and the concept of a Church Militant.

Religious faith aside, the members of an effective hunter-killer team must function within absolute articles of integrity, ethical behavior, and, most importantly, reside over the same militant spirit that drive hunters to withstand the challenges to conquer his or her prey. Only within these higher ideals can individuals strive for becoming true soldiers rather than opportunistic thugs.

Summary

The foundation of military forces remains the inherent hunter instinct within all human individuals. The ability to track prey, and spirit for the kill remains as precious as breathing air. Only when we can foster this primitive trait, can our soldiers survive within the battlefield.

CHAPTER THREE:
EFFECTIVE WARRIORS.

THROUGHOUT HISTORY, SOLDIERS have been cast into a singular grouping when, in fact, they fall into three distinct classes: conscripts, professionals, and warriors. The first group consists of those members thrust into military service for the benefit of the nation or the kingdom for which he serves. The second classification represents those rare individuals who choose to serve within the military, primarily (but not necessarily) as a career. These individuals generally serve with pride, patriotism, and professionalism – though "pirates" exist turning even the most illustrious operation sour through personal ambition and power. Lastly, we turn to the rarest of the rare, the *true warrior* whose entire life rests upon militant exceptionalism.

With populations geared towards public service shrinking at an alarming rate, professional soldiering is rapidly becoming an extinct choice of career. Nevertheless, there remains a small cadre of exceptional individuals whose lives depend upon expression as true military theorists. That is, these superior individuals bear inherent traits that *no* military organization can foster through even the toughest of basic or special forces training. When most "special" operations units train through principles of *immersion*, these Gideonesque men absorb the concepts of the warrior lifestyle seemingly from birth. And they are becoming exceedingly rare within today's ultra-technological society.

With the advent of social media, cyber networks, and loose play with everyday lives, the 'warrior spirit' dissipates from the soldiering population. More often than not, today's military men and women found themselves upon technical conveniences that do little but to segregate primal tendencies from reliance upon technical crutches. More to the point, very few young individuals today can master *any* subject without resorting to information technology as a guide, mentor, or substitute. Unfortunately, the battlefield of the future will be nowhere near as technical as are the mountains of Afghanistan or Syria today. To fight these conflicts, we need to master the basics of old; the warriors of the future will be just as lethal, just as primal, as their ancestors of the prehistoric age.

Soldiers Extraordinaire

When political push comes to military shove, few cares to possess weak diplomats. Citizens do not wish for their militaries to surrender and military personnel do no enjoy being micromanaged by distant politicians. Sadly, however, a great many armies do surrender, and a great many politicians force him or herself into strategic and tactical planning. Perhaps, this explains why some of history's greatest military minds – and more than a few despots – hailed from outside the traditional military career path.

Often, in the case, say, of the Spanish Conquistadors invading the New World, these extraordinary military talents fuel expertise with ambitions of personal profit. Others, including ancient Israelite judge Gideon, sought to conquer solely for God rather than gold. Today, at least within major national armies, we are unlikely to see soldiers fighting for either profit or religion – at least *officially*. In Western examples, the "call to serve" still reigns as the primary reason professionals choose to enter the field. How, then, are we to evaluate recruits?

Table 1. Desirable Qualities of Soldiers

	May Have	Should Have	Must Have
Intelligence			X
Commonsense			X
Creativity		X	
Initiative		X	
Inquisitiveness	X		
Mechanical Aptitude	X		
Fieldcraft			X

In Table 1, we can observe a partial list of desirable qualities for the modern soldier, for which we shall now elaborate upon. To begin, *every soldier* must posses both intelligence and commonsense; the world can no longer afford to accept mere conscripts – i.e., "bodies" – into the ranks of its largest militaries, for to do so simply attends to the attritional armies that we are trying to avoid. Unfortunately, the very concept of "intelligence" remains maligned and misunderstood. Far from mere cranial capacity (or even activity), *intelligence* implies the ability to store, retrieve, and, beyond all else, *process* information for advantage.

An intelligent person remains both a "knowledge curator" and an appreciator of that knowledge, discriminating amongst the source, period, and value of the information acquired. What *common sense* does, however, is provide a mechanism for challenging that information vis-à-vis one's gut instincts. That is, when an individual suspects that, say, "popular opinion" is wrong, then he or she acts upon their knowledge, training, and instinct alone to affect a course of action irrespective of such group think. Such divergence from the expected simply underscores that individual's belief that life has taught them a better course.

From here, we can argue that any good soldier should bear the traits of creativity and initiative. We say "should" because, frankly, creativity remains an inherent trait born into some individuals and shielded from others. For its role, initiative founds upon both inherent and environmental factors that may present themselves upon persons in varying degrees. For our purposes, however, both attributes can be cultivated – to a point.

Any person with intelligence and commonsense can be taught to develop creative-like thought processes that, while not necessarily artistic in scope, can lead to decisions and actions foreign to institutional training and doctrine. The essence of creativity, for our needs, simply means the ability to *create* – to bring about solutions, products, services, or decisions based solely upon imaginative skill. A creative personality, each to his or her own degree of familiarization, can produce outside the status quo, envision that which yet does not exist, and perceive that which *others* may consider or produce.

Initiative, as per our discussion, simply means that we desire soldiers that do not *wait* for solutions; they are prepared to act to keep from becoming stagnant. Here is where we can observe how creativity is required to foster initiative; solutions do not come by way of bureaucracy. In war, when mere seconds may determine the outcome of the future, waiting days, weeks, or months for protocol has destroyed a great many empires. In the modern era, even "instant" communications technology remains sluggish.

Mechanical ability and natural inquisitiveness can aid within the foregoing, but do not mean that militaries must rule out otherwise well-qualified soldiers. These characteristics simply permit individuals to fashion repairs and suggestions, which may lead to improvements within the operational capacity of the group. Nevertheless, almost any intelligent person can learn to repair basic equipment or discover new opportunities without these inherent traits. Therefore, practical military leaders would be advised to assign specific tasks to soldiers based upon their individual abilities.

Finally, *all* soldiers must be proficient in fieldcraft and this is where the dichotomy exists between present militaries and those required to fight future wars. No longer can we place technology-centric individuals into primitive battlefields. We must shore the primal characteristics forged within human evolution so that soldiers remain adept at confronting adversaries born and bred in cultures where, say, St. Simeon Stylites lived "uninterruptedly" for three decades atop a sixty-foot pillar no larger in circumference than your typical office chair. To simply state that *today's* soldiers no longer need to consider such archaic beliefs forfeits his or her ability to adapt to a large portion of the planet's population.

In discussing fieldcraft, we must specify by what attributes we are primarily concerned with:

- *Camouflage.* Soldiers must understand how to blend in to his or her everchanging 'natural' environment, whether this represents the rainforest or a modern urban setting. Their passage through this environment must not attract unwanted attention from either animal or human observers. In short, he or she must melt into their surroundings as effortlessly as possible.

- *Navigation.* In an age of global positioning satellites and smart phones, it may seem ridiculous to find ourselves lost *anywhere*, but proper navigation must be included within *any* person's life lest they find themselves devoted to the 'technology god' that remains as artificial as yesterday's astrolabe. Countless species routinely navigate their way across thousands of miles without any outside mechanisms other than the sun, stars, climate, terrain, and basic instinct. Soldiers can add to this such temporary measures as tying discreet knots in vines, placing stones atop one another, or simply remembering prominent patterns of trees.

- *Concealment/Cover.* Here, we are primarily discussing the ability to hide one's presence from the enemy prior to or following contact. As a broader perspective of camouflage, concealment includes such measures as reducing noise, eliminating sign, and avoiding compromise through color, shine, or shape foreign to the location. Cover involves those aspects of concealment that necessarily arise after an individual or group has been observed by the enemy, often during gunfire.

- *Obstacle crossing.* In any environment, be it forest, desert, or mountains, there will be a need to cross rivers, gullies, or scale hills. Some of these obstacles may be met with simple consideration. Others may require a great deal of planning and ingenuity. Regardless, soldiers on the move *must* understand how to pass obstructions both natural and artificial in nature.

- *Observation.* Generally, people do not move very

much when they intently study a subject. Part of this rests with the binocular vision of the species; individuals tend to relay upon the steadiness of his or her legs to bring both eyes to bear upon the object of their scrutiny. Unfortunately, this dismisses several fundamental (and primal) traits, especially peripheral vision. Soldiers must not only recognize shapes, colors, distances, and unnatural arrangements within his or her environment, they *must* be able to do so while on the move. This brings relativity within their environment, as they must learn to scrutinize surroundings while accounting for personal intrusion through that environment.

- *Countersurveillance.* Countersurveillance must go hand in hand with both observation and concealment/cover for it deals specifically with denying an enemy observer of the presence of the soldier. Here is where the foot soldier becomes a "ghost" within his environment; traveling consciously knowing what *not* to leave behind for experienced eyes to observe. It represents the culmination of fieldcraft itself.

- *Survival, Evasion, and Escape.* The very concept of operating deep behind enemy lines offers the decidedly unnerving thought of being captured and, frankly, today's adversaries very rarely consider keeping prisoners alive and intact. Therefore, *every* soldier on the battlefield must be thoroughly trained in survival (with virtually zero provisions), evading capture (with little rest), and escape from captivity. These attributes must be so ingrained into the individual's subconsciousness that they can be enacted without anxiety.

With these guidelines in mind, fieldcraft becomes the core

"undergraduate" study towards the soldier's sought after mastering of his or her profession.

With this perspective in mind, it becomes decidedly easier to affect an appropriate training regimen designed to instill a sense of the hunter into what can only be described as a killing profession.

Humanity's Most Dangerous Profession

Whether modern civilized society cares to acknowledge it or not, soldiering means killing – at a minimum, the training to potentially kill another human individual or group. It remains, very likely, society's oldest sin outside of disobedience and blaming others. From the Biblical perspective, we are confronted with a brother killing a brother within the fourth chapter of the Book (and, appropriately, the chapter following the Fall of Man). However one views the subject, killing became an instant success with those who developed jealousies and hatreds towards one another.

In our discussion, we need only concern ourselves with the organization and training of military (and paramilitary) forces, which arose out of the need to impart largescale killing upon those whose presence interfered with the plans of the aggressor or defender. As with all human endeavors, once a need was declared, people stepped forward to provide the remedy. From primitive individuals serving a local chieftain on through well-trained and disciplined soldiers serving representative politicians, militaries arose to persuade adversaries through superior strength, resolve, and lethal justice.

That many modern military forces have been thrust into such ancillary duties as peacekeeping, disaster relief, and law enforcement bears more to do with their discipline and organization rather than effectiveness within any of these fields. At their most fundamental level, militaries represent people trained with and operating weapons systems, be that a sidearm or bomber borne nuclear weapons.

Effectiveness – and excellence – within any endeavor requires the participant to focus exclusively upon that objective and, herein, military and warfare are not exceptions to the rule. Soldiers that do not excel upon the battlefield quickly become prisoners, casualties, or simply killed in action. To avoid lost of life or freedom requires an individual to engage within that most primal of human characteristics: kill or be killed.

Success on the battlefield, insofar as discussion permits, requires a complete reprogramming of the human mind; a fundamental alteration in how individuals react and respond to martial crises. Some of this is done during basic training; a great deal more during special operations group initiation. Yet, neither of these avenues serve well for the independent soldier working on initiative, cunning, and longevity. Today's military has become too bureaucratic – merely another point on the military-security-law enforcement equation.

Proper military consideration, understandably, rests within tight constrictions. It is less jurisdictional than law enforcement and far more militant. Nevertheless, militaries fall under strict legislative guidelines and international norms. That said, however, war itself represents an affront to global peace and order and therefore must fully be prosecuted (there being only one thing worse than martial conflict – *partial* military engagement under the belief that such hesitation fosters diplomacy).

In modern recorded history, perhaps, there are only two legitimate conflicts worthy of being considered as "all-out" wars: the American Civil War and World War Two. These two examples illustrate victory through absolute denial of enemy resources and should be considered even down to the frontline troop level. To achieve victory – whether considering the squad or national level – militaries must task themselves with the following goals:

1. To eliminate all direct threats against the aggressor unit;

2. To deny all support to the defending unit;

3. To erect a barrier between the defender's leadership and recruitment.

Some of these aspects may appear foreign to the military student, so we will briefly discuss them.

To eliminate all direct threats against a military unit remains Warfare 101 but is often overlooked by those commanding the units or armies in question. In the West, in particular, militaries are often assigned with limited, almost imperceptible objectives that serve little but to extend the conflict (likely until after national elections or leadership changes). Yet, war is a do or die function; once a blade is thrust, it cannot be retrieved without completing its path.

Denying support to the defender is, often, the cause for attritional style warfare. Nations try to pare one another until the adversary quits or is tempered at the polls. Nevertheless, such warfare has been around since even before Joshua's siege of Jericho and is quite effective in practice if not expedient. Another prime example of such warfare remains the first century destruction of Jerusalem. On the small unit level, however, it remains necessary simply to keep enemy patrols and squads from receiving either supplies or intelligence from local populations.

The final objective, in layman's terms, is simply to deny

the enemy an opportunity to glorify its cause – something smaller, hunter-killer units are likely to encounter in combating, say, narco-traffickers and Islamic jihadists. These groups must be isolated from the heroism and adventurism inherent within revolutionary and zealous movements likely to be found within the world's irregular battlefields. To take out these leaders remains, arguably, the greatest force-multiplier in small unit, asymmetrical warfare.

Ideally, the small unit is best served by intelligent, innovative, and inciteful individuals bred on a dogged pursuit of goals with training and experience within the undeveloped environment. Finding such personnel, sadly, represents the Achille's heel for most global military organizations – not to mention law enforcement and security operations. Too often today, organizations are faced with either what one has available or that which local legislation (and lawsuits) permit. Regardless, properly motivated and trainable personnel are still available if one knows where to look.

Many special operations forces groups tend to attract those with "outdoorsman" experiences such as hunting, fishing, hiking, and camping. Unfortunately, these experiences suggest an appreciation of the environment, but do not necessarily foretell a great deal of fortitude, especially in our technology-centric era. For instance, today's hunter, even when pursuing game with a bow, tends to avail themselves of branded camouflage, retail tree stands, scent reduction lotions, and preseason feeding. Contrast these hunters, say, with an individual that spends weeks tracking down a brown bear with a longbow.

In this discussion, for instance, we would do better to employ a technically proficient wildlife photographer than we would a familial hunter. Why? Because the photographer must approach his or her prey closer than any hunter, aligned themselves for an unobstructed "shot", and then consider the myriad of climatic conditions that would hamper a saleable image. In short, the mere photographer retains far more obstacles than any firearm-packing hunter. It is this ability to close in on prey that differentiates the amateur from the professional and, frankly, very few hunters within the Western world bear the experience of their gamekeeping ancestors.

Another group of individuals worth recruiting remain those who view their outdoor "hobbies" a bit on the obsessive side. That is, *true* amateurs within his or her field. In the traditional sense, "amateur" represents one who does his or her pastime solely out of love for the pursuit. Here, we must retain the equally traditional concept of love; one in love with *anything* holds no reservations regarding that love. In our context, one who loves a particular hobby, undertakes it unceasingly. And here is where we need to focus.

In modern society, most individuals remain superficial; they undertake any activity as long as there remains a profitable goal achieved with the least amount of exertion. We arrive at work as long as we are feeling fine and no other preoccupations thwart us. We shop with the expectation that the retailer will always have what we want in stock and there are no lines at the cash register. We attend church services on Sunday as long as we leave the building feeling as if *we gained* something from the visit. Finally, we never, *ever* voice our personal beliefs unless *everyone else* subscribes to those beliefs as well.

True amateurs, to the contrary, undertake his or her activity whether it rains or shines, whether they bear enough money or not, and whether or not they have any friends or family members supporting the hobby. In this regard, they do *whatever it takes* to get the job done – precisely the type of individual that military hunter-killer units need. Whereas someone targeting whitetail deer may, for example, select a specific date or time convenient for hunting, the amateur photographer, to the contrary, may devote weeks and months capturing the "perfect" image of a deer for sale to a magazine or stock agency. The former adds hunting to his schedule whereas the latter schedules his target to his life. There is a *profound* difference.

Due to the abject necessity of militant behavior, armies serving national communities cannot be staffed with part-time or transitory soldiers whose conscience rests on "other things" when time comes for him or her to thrust a lance into an opponent. Nor can we equip our militaries with individuals who view martial conflict as, perhaps, some videogame sequencing karate kicks, rapid weapon changes, and, most egregiously, special-order "life renewals". Real life is most emphatically *not* a videogame and its consequences are usually instantaneous and irreversible.

Effective hunter-killer operations require effective hunter-killers; individuals born and bred to undertake the most grueling tasks under the most ardent conditions under the tightest schedules possible, perhaps, in the modern military environment. Their job is to seek out and neutralize individuals that offer force-multiplication advantages through his death (despite assurances within the West, most of the world's leaders and military practitioners do not equate women as critical components within their organizations).

Due to the need for both secrecy and operational isolation, hunter-killer units remain outside the micromanagement of traditional military hierarchies and, therefore, their soldiers remain those whose independence and supply appear primitive for even well-trained special operations soldiers and snipers. These teams bear only one goal at any given time – again, to seek out and eliminate a *specific individual* regardless of the weather, conditions on the ground, and instructions from headquarters. They will *only* cease in their function when that individual has been killed, for any concept of "hunter-gatherers" must relinquish to intelligence operations that may, or may not, support the killer team in action.

Soldiering remains a deadly profession, one that cannot exist outside a nation's military forces. To engage within warfare without "just cause" response dilutes into criminality at best and terrorism at worst. Without the indiscriminate nature of either criminality or terrorism, military participation becomes, indeed, the planet's most dangerous profession if only because the element of freedom is removed from conscious decision – the soldier acts *discriminately* and only when so aroused. True soldiers kill with the acuteness of the surgeon's scalpel.

Summary

Historically, soldiers have been thrust into a uniform category that dismisses how he or she came into organizational familiarity. Henceforth, there is little discrimination into how, say, a new desk clerk differentiates from an experienced sniper. Nevertheless, as more of the world's conflicts descend back into their primitive nature, soldiers will have to become more aggressive, more discriminating, and more inherent than today's examples. He or she must be, at their most fundamental level, a *killer*, albeit one with society's best reservations at hand. To *hunt* requires one to subconsciously understand their prey and to kill manifests a deep knowledge of just how to carry out that neutralization without jeopardizing innocent bystanders.

CHAPTER FOUR:
EFFECTIVE KILLING.

AMERICAN UNION GENERAL William Tecumseh Sherman declaring that "War is hell" underscored the nature of primal conflict. Having had aided in the decimation of the South, Sherman embarked upon a decidedly pacifist postwar campaign to right the travesties of brother fighting against brother, a truly Biblical lesson. His assertion was that he fought because he *had* to fight. Even a brief inspection of his statements proves that the general abhorred war, but he also abhorred those who either glorified it or thought that it could be made more civilized.

As Sherman implied, only those who had never fired a bullet or heard the screams of the wounded thought war to be glorious and commendable. His anger was exceptional towards the newsmen of his day that, as with the present, fueled their stories largely with rumors just to score advantage with readers. This can further be argued as the fundamental reason that politicians gained unnatural control over their militaries. In Sherman's case, his nation was led by the equally rational Abraham Lincoln whose devotion to the integrity of the Union and absolute hatred of slavery permitted his generals to fight to the hilt.

Today, the aversion towards war remains solely within the planet's lay population, as the forty or so conflicts ongoing within the world at any given moment attest to conflict as a tool of politicians. Because of this dichotomy between leaders and constituents, great care must be applied within any militant activity. In brief, victory represents votes and disaster leads to scandal within *any* legislative or executive body.

This reality places military leaders and soldiers in a conundrum; they must fight to win but do so without aggravating politicians' careers. In other words, soldiers the world over face the paradox of having to do his or her job without jeopardizing that of their legislative leaders. One seeks victory at all costs; the other victory at no cost (to him or her). To kill without being killed remains preferential at the ballot box. Again, this places soldiers within a tight corner for they are required to undertake the unimaginable: eliminate the enemy without publicizing they are eliminating their enemy. War may be hell, but politics remains truly diabolical.

Getting Biblical

In discussing either human history, warfare in particular, or even religious beliefs, one cannot escape inclusion of the Bible, specifically the forty-six books (in the Roman Catholic version) of the Old Testament. In these nearly four dozen books contain the markings of humanity's greatest military excursions, fusing elements of politics, religion, national identity, and raw hatred into survival. Theologians note that the brutality of the pre-Christian era remained to prepare Israel for the arrival of Christ, and even the Gospel message of turning the other cheek rests largely within Fort McHenry-esque determination. Nevertheless, tacticians routinely peruse the pages of the Bible, particularly First and Second Maccabees, for instances of pretechnological military advantages.

In this Sacred Book, arguably the most influential library

of literary works in the world, militaries can find both the rationale and the tactics necessary to wage effective hunter-killer operations. The story of Gideon rests on the judge's selection of smaller, reliable groups rather than generic "bodies" (Judges 7:5-7). Adherence to established law and order and the purification of one's beliefs represents the basis for the Maccabees tales (see 1 Maccabees 2:39-48). And, of course, there remains Joshua's espionage efforts saved at the hands of Rahab (Joshua 2), attesting to the need for both intelligence and local support amongst small unit military tactics.

From the more modern perspective, even prior to General Sherman's personal observations, 19th Century Clausewitz wrote within his treatise *On War* that acts carried out in kindness represented the vilest of military maneuvers. The Prussian general's own opinion perhaps fostered Sherman's views, but both generals knew that once war had been declared, the gauntlets had to come off; there could be no half-measures in warfare whether ancient or modern.

In this regard, military leaders (and their political overseers) *must* conclude that military conflict remains, always, a fight for survival. Little more. To excuse combat as a "police action", "peacekeeping", or even a "War against terror" simply dilutes the fact that whatever crisis presents itself, *killing* has become the mandatory solution. Here is where, perhaps, we arrive at the crux of Biblical warfare.

Throughout the course of human history, from the Biblical Cain and Judas Iscariot, on through today's Islamic jihadists and narco-centric killers, there are *some* people that cannot be reasoned with. They will either die for his or her cause, or they will accept death because they see no other salvation within their lives. They will kill – or permit others to be killed – simply because they remain incapable of compromise. These individuals epitomize the targets of effective military hunter-killer teams, for when one cannot be reasoned with, they cannot be persuaded to surrender.

In this regard, ongoing military conflict requires that adversaries either capitulate or cease to exist. For instance, a profound narcotics distributor is not likely to acquiesce to incarceration or even dilution through the legality of drugs. He or she is more likely to find avenues around prison or legislation to retain their profitable enterprise. In consideration of this, *termination* may represent the only way to cease this individual's activities – as unpalatable as that realization may be. Civility may be compromised within politics, but it can *never* be discussed within combat.

Western armies, in particular, often fall victim to a disease rampant within the intelligence field: *mirror imaging*, the process by which individuals impart personal biases upon their analysis of others. It is how one political party, for instance, quickly libels an opposition group by any number of alleged atrocities and crimes because, at root level, it is what *the accusers* would normally do. For militaries, however, mirror imaging simply dictates that "they" would not do...because *we* would not do such. The world remains awash with the corpses of those who would not do what their adversaries were quite willing to do.

In this regard, we must now consider what the term "kill" means. In its briefest sense, to kill anything renders that object essentially useless. That is, to kill a radio, for instance, implies a desire for cessation of its sound. To kill a beverage, similarly, means to consume the contents of its container in full – and usually, very quickly. On the other hand, to kill an animal such as a deer, means to end that creature's life; eliminating its animated body. The finality of this last description rests within the occupation of military hunter-killer operations: the irreversible elimination of a target's "animated body". In other words, actionable justice of the most extreme variety.

For expediency – *all* military operations must bear a degree of expediency – we observe that there remain only two methods of ceasing an opponent's life rather effectively. Either that individual is dispatched with the most violent (i.e., explosion) or the most surgical (e.g., gunshot to the third vertebrate) method available. In between these two extremes, a human life may take a great deal of time to expire. This reality is profound within situations where, for instance, the target represents a drug-crazed or fanatical zealot wherein they may withstand several shots to the body before incapacitation occurs. Efficient military operations cannot, as with the case of U.S. ground combat soldiers in Vietnam, employ and average of 50,000 rounds to inflict a single casualty.

At worst, military forces must dispatch their adversary with no more than three shots – one to the head, two to the chest to ensure death. The headshot renders the individual unable to function as a complete person; the chest shots ensure that cardiovascular activities are disrupted. In many situations, this is the *best* that military forces may hope for as lingering within the area to ensure that the target individual is *truly* dead may lead to collateral deaths within its own ranks. As it is, such three-shot-maximum targeting requires friendly forces to move into a very close range with the adversary (far closer than most sniper operations, for comparison).

The dual objective here – possibly not available through sniper *team* operations – is both killing the individual and ensuring recordation of the kill. Where hunter-killer operations, perhaps, distance themselves most acutely from traditional sniper functions is that the hunter-killer team remains more mobile and far-ranging than sniper pairs or groups. They are not, most emphatically, 'wait and kill' operations; hunter-killer teams are inserted, move, and extract more quickly than comparable sniper operations but may also linger a bit more than conventional forces. In this regard, the entire team emerges as a "sniper package" more so than their military brethren.

Given the nature of the effective hunter-killer team – that of an independent, decentralized force inserted to take down *specific* targets within a certain period of time fully isolated from bureaucratic command structures – we can now turn the discussion towards how to infuse these properties in with expected military operations. That is, where do we most effectively divert from (and assimilate into) what could be considered as traditional sniper operations. In this regard, one could draw the conclusion that such operations divert from sniper functions in that, insofar as possible, hunter-killer teams are assembled *for specific targets*; meaning that components of intelligence, armament, logistics, and linguistics may arise for that one operation only, whereas many – if not most – sniper operations employ individuals trained within traditional sniper-scout functions.

Furthermore, hunter-killer teams may be required to track their target across multiple borders, through multiple environments, and employ multiple opportunities that, perhaps, more clandestine sniper groups may avoid. Here, we are leaning more towards a running pack of wolves rather than the quickness of a rattlesnake's thrust. Or, far more likely, the difference between a group of ninjas as opposed to samurai. The latter seeks the perfect strike to subdue his opponent whereas the former seeks to eliminate his opponent's function as much through terror as through sinister force.

In summation, effective hunter-killer teams render actionable justice upon their opponents; meaning, largely, that in true Biblical fashion, their objective remains to *permanently* cease the function (lives) of extraordinarily motivated individuals whose incapacitation renders operational insolvency within their whole organization. In a broader – if somewhat blasphemous in slant – consideration, these hunter-killer teams bring about the "Wrath of God" often declared in battle, but rarely instituted. More of Sherman's decimating the South rather than General George R. Crook's relative pacification of Native Americans during his exploits in the post-Civil War era of the American West.

Merciless Killing versus Killing Mercilessly

Politicians in general, and the media in particular, remain forces that forever seek to civilize war. One group remains aghast at war in order to shore votes while the other seeks to gain readership through their arguments (now largely) against conflict. Oddly, it remains liberal Hollywood that often displays the most violent action through its movies and television shows where armaments produce the most spectacular – and visually entertaining if not technically accurate – effects. All three groups fail miserably in addressing the fundamental root of *all* military conflicts: killing.

The fine line between killing for survival and killing for opportunity often expands past a recalcitrant population concerned more about financial obligations and leisure activity than he or she is about thwarting wolves baying at the door. Yet, we see this frivolous demarcation whenever we read the evening news or inquire of our favorite social media site. Accordingly, we equate terrorists with "freedom fighters", Constitutionalists with neo-Nazis, and conscientious voters with bigots. Dilution of facts has become an American (and Western) pastime. Nevertheless, this preoccupation with redefinition remains deadly upon the battlefield.

In war, militaries must kill and during peacetime they must relentlessly practice killing in war. Anything less than these two activities remains an affront to countless veterans who died serving his or her nation. That the world often minimalizes the concept of killing within battle necessarily leads to more indiscriminate killing in subsequent wars. And populations become immune to that which they do not adequately address. The rise of violent video games, it has frequently been argued, leads to rise in violence across urban landscapes in many "civilized" nations simply because our youth has become desensitized to the fact that, in real life, killing does not come with a reset button or life extension credits.

Here, within our discussion regarding effective hunter-killer operations, we must finalize our treatment of the word 'to kill' lest we forever descend into semantics. When we speak of killing enemy soldiers (or even key civilian employees or contractors) on the battlefield or other militant environments, we are not suggesting indiscriminate mayhem. Far from it. We are merely employing the form of 'Just War' that differentiates targets based upon their being *no other legitimate means* to cease that individual's killing of innocent personnel and friendly military forces. That is, if only *they* would cease killing themselves, then *we* would have no cause to target them for death.

More importantly, *our* targeting rests upon those individuals whose death fosters a greater focus upon peace rather than needlessly killing enemy soldiers merely serving out his or her enlistment or conscription. Ours, again, is not an attritional duty, but a force multiplication argument resting upon *who* to kill rather than simply accounting for body bags and daily television kill ratios. In fact, due to the highly secretive lifestyles of most high-value targets (HVT), it remains unlikely that his death will generate any media attention at all. At least not as timely as, say, terrorist attacks or largescale battles of the WWII variety.

Amputations always garner a greater share of notoriety than simple dissection, but such limb removals often come as either a last resort or a reaction to previous malpractice.

Yet, such malpractice in war can lead to endless years of accusations regarding genocide, atrocity, and similar venues for war crimes commissions. Whichever accusation presents itself, it does not bode well for clandestine or covert military operations.

In effective military operations, killing *must* be undertaken concisely, without waste of time or energy, and the result must possess significant – and otherwise unobtainable – goals for the aggressor nation. Retreating for a moment to General Sherman's "March to the Sea", his troops' killing – both in the human colloquial and within the broader operational or spiritual – of troops ushered in the 'end' for Confederate resistance towards remaining within the Union. This was achieved by sapping it of the very foundation of human existence: life itself.

Targeting human beings for killing remains the toughest job for *any* military or paramilitary force to handle. Despite the primal nature of humans killing humans, the modern (largely Western) world rests upon a firm foundation of the Golden Rule. Accordingly, most people alive today would rather surrender than attempt to force any measure of martial response towards what can only be considered as national, military objectives.

To achieve these objectives, the military team must consider the following:

1. ***Intelligence Analysis.*** Has enough information been obtained and analyzed that permits military leadership sufficient data to *accurately* predict the advantages of targeting the individual(s) in question. That is, has this analysis proved beyond a reasonable doubt that such targeting will irreparably harm the enemy's capacity to wage war against friendly forces.

2. **Target Accessibility.** Can a properly trained and self-sufficient military team reach and reconnoiter the targeted individual(s) within a given period of time (say, no more than 14 days)? In other words, what are the chances that the hunter-killer team can locate, identify, and position themselves for the kill based upon the mobility and environmental position of the target.

3. **Team Assembly.** Can such a trained team be assembled from individuals on hand? It remains imperative that hunter-killer teams be comprised of the best available personnel *for the mission at hand* and all perceived requirements. As these needs change over time and situation, it is not prudent to apply these requirements to existing groups of personnel. Rather, each specific mission must be staffed according to its own guidelines.

4. **Method of killing**. Given the nature of hunter-killer teams in general, it is not advisable to discuss methods of killing in the abstract. Nevertheless, the root goal of each team's mission remains to *kill* an individual or individuals whose death *leads to the quick cessation of war*. Regardless, military forces do not earn the appreciation of non-combatants if they, say, destroy an entire city block just to kill a single individual. In this regard, effective hunter-killer teams must address the issue of "tools" within their role for, perhaps, operations within an urban environment may require a fundamentally different way of terminating a target than one would encounter in the rainforest.

These requirements can be discussed further employing two brief case studies.

Although not specifically a hunter-*killer* operation, per se, the hunt for Nazi war criminal Adolf Eichmann by Israel's nascent Mossad intelligence service offers much to be considered. Here we have the epitome of a dedicated, intelligence-centric hunt for an elusive prey, someone directly responsible for the deaths of millions of Jews during the Second World War. Once intelligence had isolated the Nazi in Argentina, a tightknit "capture" team was assembled based upon the specific requirements of locating, abducting, secreting, and exporting a *specific individual* from within a distant, foreign land. That the Mossad operation bore relatively limited resources and had to employ substantial local support underscores the problems facing any military team set on *killing* its target rather than merely whisking the individual away for public trial. There is little doubt that this operation should be required study for military hunter-killer teams and their leadership.

The second case study involves the far more brutal – and, henceforth, "industrial" – search for and killing of narcotics kingpin Pablo Escobar in Colombia. A nominally combined effort by American special forces, the Colombian police Search Bloc unit, and vigilante *Los Pepes* operations led to the trafficker's location and ultimate demise. Unfortunately, this case proves the necessity of refraining from "all out" warfare in matters of tracking specific targets as numerous innocent bystanders were killed and injured during the process. More specifically, the hunt for Escobar bore little appreciation of surgical efforts and largely represented an attritional style conflict merely scaled down into replicative violence.

Effective operations must be economical ones as well and herein rests the crux of hunter-killer teams – extremely efficient, decidedly aggressive, and functionally violent groups that can seek out, identify, categorize, and neutralize high-value targets leading directly to the termination of ongoing hostilities. Nothing must be wasted, especially innocent lives whose destruction seems to remain prominent within national or terroristic campaigns. Such actions represent the most singularly focused military operations within any form of martial conflict.

Without true and accurate discrimination, hunter-killer operations descend into little more than simply targeting whomever remains available for killing; actions best left for bureaucratic institutions whose constituent power permits them to offset any accusations of impropriety or scandal.

Summary

For the entire course of human history, killing one's adversaries has always been a viable option, one marginally diluted during the rise of Christian ethics and modern, progressive politics. Nevertheless, the primacy of this option has given way towards indiscriminate murder on the battlefields of the planet. Killing for the sake of killing further leads to the attritional conflicts that plague progress and hamper peace. To counter this, martial actions *must* combine the sincerity of violence with the focus of appreciation. In other words, killing one's opponent must foster both consideration of merit and implementation of specifics designed to ensure that the act of neutralizing enemy personnel does not force casualties beyond the battlefield.

CHAPTER FIVE:
SUMMATION OF ACTION.

MILITARY HUNTER-KILLER TEAMS operate within that twilight world dominated by actionable intelligence and applied justice, most unnoticeable within the modern world. That is, they represent groups organized with the singular purpose of tracking down and killing *specific* individuals regardless of location or timeframe. Consciously more lethal than traditional military forces, these units bear more discretion than, perhaps, comparable scout-sniper units whose training and application bear more restrictions.

In this context, military hunter-killer teams envision a more dynamic, more lethal application of force multiplication than normal; a desire to seek out and eliminate accountable personalities that, it remains hoped, will shorten the duration of any armed conflict. An admirable goal, rest assured. Nevertheless, such discretionary conflicts often rest secured on the planning board and rarely make it out into operational reality. To counter this discrepancy, we must briefly outline *how* to gauge such hunter-killer operations (noting that each *specific* mission requires equally specific considerations). From this perspective, presumably, the student and practitioner of hunter-killer operations can gain new insight into the challenges and solutions that manifest themselves.

In this narrative, we shall briefly discuss the most exceptional cases possible and refrain from endless counter-analyzes, while still permitting the reader an opportunity to place him or herself into the situations discussed.

Expedited Takedowns

Figure 4. What keeps every tyrant, criminal, terrorist, or thug awake at night. © 2018, R. J. Godlewski, *All Rights Reserved.*

Operation 'Spring of Youth', Beirut, Lebanon, April 9 1973[5]

In retaliation for the September 5, 1972 Munich Olympics terrorism attack orchestrated by the Black September wing of Yasir Arafat's Al Fatah (the largest operational group within the Palestinian Liberation Organization), which ultimately led to the death of 11 Israeli athletes, the State of Israel, under the leadership of Prime Minister Golda Meir, elected to pursue an assassination campaign to eliminate such threats against her nation. Specifically, this coordinated effort enacted revenge upon those directly responsible for the highly publicized Munich attack.

Israel's Mossad (*Mossad Merkazi Le-modiin U-Letafkidim*

---

[5] See Klein, Aaron J., *Striking Back* (New York: Random House, 2005), 157-170.

Meyuhadim – Central Institute for Intelligence and Security) intelligence service led the nation's counterterrorism operations with the Israel Defense Force's (IDF) *Sayeret Matkal* ("The Unit" – General Staff Reconnaissance Unit 269) commando group serving as Israel's sword for enacting justice.

The operation targeted three particular individuals, Muhammad Yussef Najar, a founding member of Fatah, Kamal Adwan an engineer and commander of the Fatah unit created to attack Israel on its own soil, and PLO spokesman, Kamal Nasser, a Palestinian Christian. To assassinate these individuals, Israel sent sixteen commandos ashore from naval missile boats supported by several Mossad agents operating within Beirut as tourists and army units conducting diversionary operations throughout the city.

The sixteen Sayeret Matkal operatives arrived ashore dressed as "husband and wife" teams, each respective partner wearing wigs, dresses, and bras to conceal their true identity. Once on Lebanese soil, the commandos met with the "tourists" parked in three rental Buick Skylarks, which transported the assault teams to their final destination. Using a mix of explosive entry and gunfire, the Israeli commandos succeeded in killing their targets before making a relatively safe retreat to the waiting gunboats.

Far from being a silent effort, the Israeli commando raid in Beirut ushered in more than terror for the terrorists; it succeeded in causing a great deal of collateral damage and attention for the practitioner to consider. First, Adwan was killed in front of his wife and children – a reprehensible action for any "professional" soldier. Second, Najar, also known as Abu-Yussef, had been shot repeatedly through a closed door, an action that fatally killed his wife as well. This is more incomprehensible than killing someone in full view of their family.

Beyond the killing of the terrorists and one's spouse, the Israeli raid further killed an innocent Italian woman, who was seventy-one years old and merely acted as a curious (to the commotion) neighbor and several Lebanese police officers whose Land Rover vehicle received a hand grenade courtesy one of the commandos.

From the perspective of revenge and intimidation, the Israeli commando raid into Beirut brilliantly served its purpose. However, from the professional and public relations point of view, it suffered heavily. At best, it remained an operation that could be considered as successful within the context of Israel's broader counterterrorism strategy, but weak in regard to the clandestine nature of effective hunter-killer operations in general. We shall now elaborate a bit more fully.

Amphibious military operations – as opposed to, say, airborne deployments – are inherently more effective in transporting soldiers and other combatants when coastal insertion is possible. Israel's choice of landing commandos upon a private beach during a cold and windy night assured its troops of reaching their objective unseen. Dressing as both men and woman out for a walk within an otherwise cosmopolitan city further diluted any consideration by potential observers.

That these forces were met by prepositioned operatives and supported by a lengthy intelligence gathering and reconnaissance program – managed by Caesarea, Mossad's operational unit designated for conducting special missions and undercover agents within foreign territory – ensured their success in killing the PLO terrorists. Militarily speaking, this operation remains a qualified success. Nevertheless, this operation, from the perspective of hunting, reminds one of the driving (or "dogging") of deer by recreational hunters; the effect was to channel noise and threat levels to move other prey from their hide.

Table 2. Analysis of Operation Spring of Youth.

	SUCCESSES	FAILURES
PREPLANNING	Operational intelligence gathering was exemplary. Routes through the city were meticulously planned and photographs were obtained of all facilities. Local habits were also duly noted.	Collateral damage and civilian casualties appear to have been dismissed in favor of ensuring success. Targeting a residential building in a city of over one million inhabitants warrants greater care for civilian casualties.
SUPPORT	Israeli support operations remain legendary. The commandos bore the equipment, training, and logistics required of all such military operations.	Communications between the attacking force and offshore leadership were hampered (for 1973, quite understandably). One tactical radio was damaged simply by crowding too many commandos into a Buick.
EXECUTION	By most standards, the execution of the raid was flawless. The commandos assaulted their target, killed the terrorists, and hastily retreated.	Unfortunately, the violence imparted along with the resulting collateral damage give the raid a mixed critique. Once enacted, this raid was more of an ambush than a covert hunter-killer operation.
EXTRACTION	Given the violence of the action, the extraction towards the sea earns more recognition than should its insertion.	The operation unnecessarily placed local support personnel in greater day due to the chaos and commotion the attack unleashed.
OUTCOME	The Israelis set out to accomplish what they intended to. They killed three of the Munich planners and made terrorist leaders paranoid.	By exposing their intent and capabilities, Israel pushed targets into hiding and negated any "soft target" opportunities. Global opinion waned.

Operation Spring of Youth offers several key recommendations in the positive and negative aspects of effective hunter-killer operations (See Table 2). Israel triumphed immeasurably in telegraphing both its intent and capabilities, but also shored the opinion that the nation remained little more than terroristic itself. This aggravated any sympathy that Israel gained from, say, conditions made known regarding the Holocaust. Nevertheless, the operation made known to the world that Israel would, without doubt, hunt down and kill *anyone* that harmed any of its citizens.

Assassination of Admiral Isoruku Yamamoto, Solomon Islands, April 18, 1943[6]

The surprise attack upon the U.S. Naval Base located at Pearl Harbor, Hawaii on the morning of December 7th, 1941 ushered in America's most costly and deadly war within its history. The unannounced attack infuriated and galvanized a nation as had few other conflicts in human history. This, the last of America's declared wars, thrust U.S. warfare into an environment that the nation had not seen since the conclusion of its Civil War three-quarters of a century before.

America's ego – and sense of security – had been crippled, but the attacks in Hawaii did little to diminish U.S. industrial or intelligence capabilities. Within a few months, the codebreaking abilities of the U.S. permitted it to exact revenge upon the Japanese fleet in May 1942, decimating the fleet that had been primed for the "...largest ambush in history" at Midway by being ambushed itself. Yet, inasmuch as American intelligence capabilities permitted itself to divert another "sneak attack" upon its vaunted fleet, it also permitted the U.S. to counter with yet another history-

---

[6] See Richelson, Jeffrey T., *A Century of Spies* (New York: Oxford University Press, 1995), 180-184.

altering attack that caught its Japanese enemy off guard.

On April 13, 1943 U.S. communications intelligence (COMINT) stations intercepted a coded message that provided a precise itinerary for Admiral Yamamoto's planned inspection of several key bases off Bougainville in the Solomon Islands. The opportunity remained too good to pass up; the orchestrated killing of an exemplary naval officer widely regarded as Japan's best ever. U.S. Admiral Chester Nimitz and his chief intelligence officer, Captain Edwin T. Layton decided to embark upon the hunt.

During the morning of April 18, when Yamamoto's airplane, covered by nine Mitsubishi Zeros, entered airspace near Kahilin they were met with the presence of eighteen American P-38 Lightnings, four of the dual engine fighters breaking off combat to pounce upon the Japanese transport. Captain Thomas G. Lamphier strafed the Admiral's plane with 20mm cannon fire, sending the doomed transport into the jungle below, killing everyone aboard. The mastermind behind the disastrous Pearl Harbor attack and the architect of many more plans died the victim of prowling hunters and superior intelligence advantages.

Three universal characteristics make this action worthy of study by anyone associated with military hunter-killer team operations. First, the timely interpretation of intelligence offered the U.S. military an *opportunity* to affect the outcome of a global conflict through the *precision targeting* of a single individual whose death warranted greater prospects for success. Second, the opportunity itself fell into the hands of those who could *appreciate* the chance to change history at the expense of an adversarial individual. Finally, the attack was launched under *a specific timeline*, meaning, of course, that the target held control over the scheduling as opposed to, say, offensive planners; the Americans bore only five days from opportunity to execution – a very brief period even in the days before the Internet.

	SUCCESSES	**FAILURES**
PREPLANNING	Restricted largely to wartime intelligence gathering, the attack on Yamamoto's plan gave the Americans only five days in which to organize an attack at the furthest perimeter with the only plane in its arsenal able to do so.	Due to the constricted schedule and distance involved, the U.S. had to send a larger than (perhaps) recommended force to ensure success. Such a fleet might have tipped off Japanese observers.
SUPPORT	U.S. intelligence intercepts provided planners with an *accurate* itinerary of Yamamoto's inspection tour including the relative number of aircraft traveling with him. This gave the strike force advantage of fact.	Japan had been in the process of altering its cryptographic code. This would have not only affected the Midway Island outcome but prevented the U.S. from attacking Yamamoto. Luck is not beneficial.
EXECUTION	Using, arguably, the best WWII plane ever, the Americans carried out the attack with the skill of a seasoned hunter: lying in wait at the *optimal* location with the *perfect* weapon for the task at hand.	Even with the best fighter available and, perhaps, a top-notch crew, the U.S. extended its reach beyond limits considered advisable. Much rested upon luck and things going "as planned", never good in battle.
EXTRACTION	The size and surprising nature of the U.S. attack aided in the crews getting back to safety.	Again, the distances involved placed undue challenges upon the flight crews and their mission.
OUTCOME	The death of Admiral Yamamoto remained an incalculable blow to Japan from which its highly-centralized military could not recover from.	Simply removing a superior opponent does not necessarily equate into gaining in wisdom or talent. There could be "others" to fill the void.

Table 3. Analysis of the Assassination of Admiral Yamamoto.

Table 3 illustrates the merits and demerits of the attack upon

Admiral Yamamoto's aircraft. This strike epitomizes the essence of hunter-killer operations, whether ground forces moving in for the kill of a terrorist or airborne force lingering around to prey upon an unsuspecting transport. In either regard, the fighter crews had to rely upon initiative, an inherent understanding of the mechanisms involved, and reliance upon using the environment for advantage. For their role, the Japanese "prey" could not foresee that their communications had been compromised, supported the admiral with potentially an inadequate escort force, and adhered to the schedule too well (an hour's delay, say, may have thwarted the ambush while not seriously compromising the admiral's inspection tour).

Filipino Pseudo-Operation against Huks, Luzon, Philippines, April 1948.[7]

The ending of the Second World War with the surrender of Japan in 1945, unleashed several prominent challenges upon the global stage. First, the victors of the conflict – largely representing the United States and its Western allies versus the always paranoid and suspicious Soviet Union – began to dissect the planet along ideological lines. Second, a great many "lesser" nations and groups realized that even the vaunted U.S. *could* be beaten, as was proven by the case of Japan's heretofore march throughout the Western and Southern Pacific. Finally, declared wars merely gave way to Western/Soviet proxy battles where free market capitalism fought against centralized communism.

Into this environment emerged the newly independent, Republic of the Philippines, a largely Roman Catholic island nation pot marked with various communist and Islamic groups seeking their own rule. One of these groups

---

[7] See Gatchel, Theodore L., "Pseudo Operations – A Double-Edged Sword of Counterinsurgency" in *Armed Groups: Studies in National Security, Counterterrorism, and Counterinsurgency,* edited by Jefferey H. Norwitz (Newport: U.S. Naval War College, 2008), 61-72.

represented the formerly anti-Japanese and proudly
communistic *Hukbalahap* or more colloquially referred to as
the "Huks" whose home rested in Central Luzon while several
relatively independent, yet similar groups operated in the
south.

During April 1948, word was received by the main Huks
that their southern brethren had engaged within a gun battle
with a group involving the Philippine Constabulary and
received casualties. A few days later, this southern Huk force
arrived in camp with two injured soldiers. After several days
of suspicion and interrogation, the northern Huk
organization finally accepted the newly arrive forces and
began sharing intelligence and field support amongst
themselves.

Nevertheless, to the startled surprise of the Huk forces in
the north, the southern "Huks" were anything but; they
represented an elite commando unit from the Constabulary
known as Force X and this counterguerrilla organization
opened fire on their enemy, killing 82 Huks including three
prominent commanders. The Huks had been deceived by a
pseudo operation – "actions in which specially trained and
equipped counterinsurgency forces disguise themselves as
insurgent bands in order to gain intelligence, carry out
attacks against insurgent forces or facilities, capture or kill
insurgent leaders, and conduct psychological operations
against the insurgents."[8] Such deception works well within a
host of military operations.

The planning within any such endeavor remains of
paramount importance, for to assume the identity of the
enemy – in either active martial or passive spy operations, as
well as purely educational "red team" exercises – requires one

---

[8] Ibid, 62.

to act, think, and *produce* as if the enemy. Not many organizations are able to do so effectively. Many Western military (and law enforcement, for that matter) personnel, in particular, struggle to view the world from any perspective other than his or her own personal biases.[9] The Force X team was sufficiently trained to withstand several days' worth of interrogation by the hostile group.

Conversely, such an operation could not reasonably assume that they could target *specific* individuals, let alone any intelligence-derived leader. Their role remained more of an internal ambush rather than a raid. Still, they succeeded in killing 82 enemy personnel, which probably could not have been killed as effectively from the outside. Furthermore, it remains probable that the Force X personnel employed intuition and common sense when their pseudo force "turned" on their hosts.

Irregular groups are, by nature, inherently xenophobic and highly suspicious of outsiders entering their territory. Penetration, therefore, cannot come by way of idle simulation. To successfully enter a hostile group, one must adequately "prepare the battlefield" and in the case of Force X, they were able to telegraph the battle where their own soldiers were injured. Unfortunately, today, militaries do not have the luxuries afforded by 1948's lack of technology; today, word – and intelligence – can be spread at the literal speed of light.

Twenty-first century hunter-killer operations must focus upon raids more than pseudo operations if they are to be successful and this negates too much time spent transforming themselves into what they are not.

---

[9] This problem is covered very well in Sloan, Stephen and Robert J. Bunker, *Red Teams and Counterterrorism Training* (Norman, OK: University of Oklahoma Press, 2011), 72-90.

	SUCCESSES	FAILURES
PREPLANNING	As a legitimate pseudo operation, Force X planners remained meticulous in preparing their soldiers for the role as "Southern Huks" escaping from a battle with Filipino government forces.	Due to the nature of the operation, it remains unlikely that Force X personnel knew *who* and *when* to launch their attack against. Therefore, this operation rested on opportunity more than, perhaps, direct action.
SUPPORT	Substantial support was required to successfully infiltrate a hostile group. Mannerisms, language, dress, etc. had to match what the Huks expected an affiliated group to present and, still, this took days to achieve.	Communication between Force X and its base of operations could not have been achieved so as not to tip off the Huks. This undoubtedly kept the group from receiving timely (and pertinent) intelligence.
EXECUTION	The execution of the operation served its purpose; a pseudo group was successfully absorbed into a hostile camp where it could do the most damage. Force X remained the instigator of the final battle.	Success, sometimes, comes too well. This would have hampered subsequent operations due to word spreading about the efforts of the Filipino government to infiltrate hostile groups.
EXTRACTION	Having bested the Huks, Force X was able to extract themselves within a conventional manner.	Egress from *any* battle involves far more considerations than insertion.
OUTCOME	The success of Force X led to ever larger and more frequent pseudo operations aiding in defeating the insurgency by ~1954.	Conversely, the Huks grew weary of large groups and so Force X (subsequently 'A-H' – á la Huk) had to rely upon smaller and more risky operations.

Table 4. Analysis of Force X pseudo operation against Huks.

Hunter-Killer operations, by necessity, remain rather defined and coordinated. While they *may* employ deception to gain access to certain groups and individuals, their role remains more clandestine than covert, more practical than obscure. In this regard, excessive attention towards deception remains adverse to the relative speed and surprise they intend to impart.

Force X was able to infiltrate the Huk compound because they imposed an elaborate ruse of suffering a battle with Filipino government forces. Having thus been "decimated" by the enemy, they embarked upon a retreat towards the northern insurgent forces under the guise of camaraderie. This remained decidedly risky; the Huks were naturally suspicious of any interlopers and once the ambush had been sprung – timing not one of optimal value – other Huk groups would become even more suspicious of outside groups.

That the forces of the Philippines were able to orchestrate more pseudo operations similar to the one discussed above has, undoubtedly, more to do with communications capabilities circa 1948 than they do about planning and execution. Similar ruses today, likely, will not have such long-term opportunities. Rather, in the 21st century, we can expect infiltration activities to remain more individualistic and expose more absorption rather than acceptance upon the part of the penetrated group.

This said, deception operations remain a valuable tool within the hunter-killer's repertoire, permitting momentary confusion upon the enemy that may mean the difference between success and failure. In the above situation, if practiced today (2018), the Force X team may have only had mere seconds to approach the Huk compound given the realities of the Internet and mobile data communications. Likely, the opposing force of Huks would have long since been advised that the "battle" within the south had been a hoax. At a minimum, they would have likely received detailed images of the combat scene and an approximate estimate of casualties and survivors.

It is exceedingly unlikely that ghost forces, such as Force X, would have prevailed long enough to fashion any kind of ambush from within the compound. Rather, their action would resort to a raid more along the lines of what true hunters present when, say, entering a riparian environment stocked with curious deer.

Summary

Effective hunter-killer operations rest upon decisive, well-choreographed, and exceptionally lethal forces supported by freedom of execution, actionable intelligence, and deception. These operations border upon the pseudo function of primary military forces engaging within paramilitary chaos. That is, by most standards, hunter-killer teams dispense with the uniformity of practiced martial exercises to elude the observation of paranoid hostile forces. In this regard, hunter-killer teams may appear as elite special operations forces, married couples on vacation, or as familial hostiles seeking refuge from government forces.

CONCLUSION:
ACTIONABLE JUSTICE.

THE MOST LETHAL century in human history has now given way to, perhaps, the most paradoxical on record. Gone, for the moment, is the East-West Cold War that pitted one hemispherical ideology against another, itself a state of eternal unrest that matured after the decimation of global fascism under the auspices of Imperial Japan, Nazi Germany, and Fascist Italy. Today's Hitlers, Mussolinis, and Tojos are less noticeable, more "businesslike" than their predecessors.

Whereas the defeat of Germany, Italy, and Japan during the 1940s came with little surprise, the collapse of the Soviet Union as the 1990s arrived certainly did. The Stalinist pressure valve that kept the world on edge for over half a century effectively disengaged, catching the entire planet off guard with fantastical realizations of "peace within our time" as despotism relegated itself to tiny hermit kingdoms such as North Korea and religiously zealous tyrannies such as Iran.

Yet, as we have seen, warfare – especially *brutal* warfare – remains as human as love, as personable as friendship, as evolutionary as languages. The desire to kill and destroy runs rampant through the human genome system, perhaps representing, in its own quaint way, the very definition of Original Sin. At best, human competitiveness, designed to foster a sense of survival and strength, ensures that some people will want to kill others. Only the methodologies have changed.

We may, God willing, never witness another Auschwitz, Nanking, or Stalingrad. Yet, we *do* bear witness to Darfur, Rwanda, and Syria. The Soviet Politburo has given way to Russian gangsters. Imperial Japan has given way to Islamic jihadism. Hitler's enthusiasm has given way to progressive absurdism. All ancient enemies paraded before our eyes under modern – and some not so modern – disguises.

What the world remains confronted with is not some seemingly inconceivable enemy hellbent on suicide, but cold, calculating "realists" who live for the day when they can destroy all those who disagree with his or her image of paradise. In this regard, the Islamic jihadist, narcotics trafficker, and popular anarchist remain as viable as ever. Only the technology employed ushers in any degree of change.

Despite these untold millions of violent perpetrators, there exists comparatively few that lead the others into action; a very few people whose energy, devotion, and influence warrant consideration by the world's intelligence and military forces. These prominent individuals – though he or she may remain somewhat concealed – propel their followers into courses of action that appear quite irrational to so-called "civilized" peoples of the world. Nevertheless, what they impart upon the planet can best be described within a solitary word: evil.

Inasmuch as the eye cannot generate its own light, the ear its own sound, or the heart its own blood, human violence cannot come from within the solitude of the human mind. External forces, combined with the relative weakness of some individual's will, push people beyond the conformity of expected behavior. Greed, lust, envy, jealousy, and ambition serve as miniscule excuses for what drives some people fanatical with violence.

The capture of Final Solution architect Adolf Eichmann,

for instance, greatly troubled many of the Israeli operatives from that mission. Here, they saw, the epitome of contrasts: the accused orchestrator of the deaths of millions of Jews appearing as little more than a meek postal clerk. This was made manifest because the individual in question – the very much unrepentant Eichmann – had been forced out of his element and into abject squander in Argentina.

Without the shield of group absolution, even the most vicious of human individuals becomes relatively meek and shallow. Without his Nazi SS authority and Germany's unchallenged power, Eichmann remained little more than a tin despot, albeit one with the stain of millions' blood upon his hands. When the 'spirit' of consolidated evil had been shattered by unified democracies, Hitler's henchman dissolved into prisoners, the hanged, and, in the case of Eichmann, blue-collar fugitives.

From the military perspective, this sudden postwar transformation remains unnerving, for it suggests that "prewar" escalations remain as sudden. So, too, is the realization that most of the world's despots – Napoleon Bonaparte, Adolf Hitler, Josef Stalin, Saddam Hussain, even Alfonso Capone – hailed from impoverished backgrounds. Fueled by evil, it does not take very long for an individual to disrupt the course of history. So, what are democracies supposed to do?

We know from the precepts of just war doctrine that allowances are made for those situations that bear *no foreseeable outcome* other than direct military action. Nevertheless, even "just" military actions require the precision of a surgeon; collateral damage *always* dilutes justice in the eyes of the law or of public opinion. An "eye for an eye" is one thing, but an entire city block for that eye reeks of blaspheme.

Once confronted with an aggressor, the defender has but

only one solution: kill or be killed. Semantics aside, discussions of apprehension and incarceration remain ludicrous on the battlefield – especially if the aggressor represents the sort of individual who cannot be reasoned with. Again, some individuals just do *not* contemplate oppositional opinions.

Adolf Eichmann, as an example, never was a soldier. His power came by way of the Reich and its absolute demand for loyalty. It was inconceivable for Nazis that their "Thousand year" empire would ever collapse to the point of responsibility for actions. In a morbid way, Nazism remained little more than a vicious, brutal, fraternity party where the participants remained intoxicated on expectations of glory. Blinded to the industrial might of America and the resolve of Great Britain, Germany feasted upon smaller nations that had long since given up on fighting for prestige.

Contrast the postwar timidity of Eichmann with the Palestinian teenager that bragged on live television about castrating his victims before gouging their eyes out or the narcotics traffickers that routinely roll severed heads across dance floors to send messages to opponents. As heinous as their actions were, Nazis still maintained the semblance of working towards building a "civilization". Today's thugs care less about nations or governments; they seek profits or prophets. The larger their world view – and their role within it – the less likely they are to remain earthbound in their means.

That many Nazis, for instance, held escape plans or provisions to "offer" their services to foreign intelligence organizations suggest that they were not bent on self-destruction the way many militants are today. A fugitive, by nature, remains a *survivor*. Not so the religious or drug-frenzied militant. The former sees the world as a temporary "proving ground" of sorts whereas the latter only observes the transitory world of his intoxication. Neither cares about international norms or social welfare.

Retreating to the case of St. Simeon Stylites that lived for thirty *uninterrupted* years atop a sixty-foot pillar no wider than a kitchen chair, letting maggots feast upon the flesh where the ropes bound into his skin, one has to reckon with such resolve within decidedly *unholy* personages. That is, for instance, combine the perseverance of St. Simeon with, say, the money of an Osama bin Laden, and the brutality of a Pablo Escobar and, well, what exists *then*?

Can the world accommodate the presence of such an evil mastermind? And what of his (or her) followers and disciples? Where does society draw the line between appreciation of apprehension and acquiescence towards annihilation? Will it take another six million (or 30 million in the case of the Soviet Union) dead to foster a sense of urgency upon the governments of the world? That much rests in the hands of the global electorate.

Our discussion, within this text, remains the development of military hunter-killer teams, specialized units charged with the tracking and termination of high-value targets that, at a minimum, reduce the effectiveness of these types of omnipresent threats. That the death of Pablo Escobar, for instance, merely led to the dispersal of cocaine trafficking does not diminish the need to target *specific* individuals. This, however, it can be argued, rests with the fault of Colombian (and American) authorities to confront subsequent traffickers with equal justice.

Military hunter-killer teams are not intended to operate as law enforcement units anymore than they are intended to function as infantry groups. Rather, their function is most emphatically *not* soldiering in the sense that they parade their uniforms at home and display them properly on the battlefield. The violence of the 21st century has dispensed with much of the protocols of the Geneva Conventions.

Hunter-killer teams exist to hunt *and* kill; they bear no provisions or interests in grabbing any available prisoners for interrogation.

Table 5. Comparison between infantry and hunter-killer assets.

	INFANTRY SOLDIERS	HUNTER-KILLER TEAMS
MISSION	To serve within the armed forces of a nation and to undertake those functions guided by international or domestic legislation during periods of conflict or peace as defined by that nation's leadership.	To seek out and terminate high-value targets deemed irrevocably hostile to their nation, its citizenry, and allied nations.
TRAINING	Vertical training in firearms, deployment, and leadership roles as required by individual soldier's position, rank, and unit designation.	Horizontal training in diverse firearms, tracking, fieldcraft, creativity, explosives, linguistics, survival and escape, surveillance, and espionage.
ORGANIZATION	Centralized command structure with (in the West) noncommissioned officers bearing the brunt of unit cohesion and adherence. Deployments undertaken via national legislative will.	Independent command structure emphasizing small unit discretion and mobility. "Launch and forget" operations once deployed.
OPERATION	Conventional military deployment with emphasis on territory acquisition and defense.	Highly deployable missions under covert and overt description with target elimination as priority over territory.

Towards this end, such teams dispense with the conventional military philosophy of drilling, marching, and reliance upon massive logistical support. As hunters, these teams excel at reading the terrain and understanding nature.

As killers, they embark upon a mission *knowing* that theirs represents a martial outcome. While some actionable intelligence may be gained during their mission, hunter-killer teams remain users of intelligence, *not collectors*. In other words, information of opportunity may be taken, but they are not sent into the field to obtain that information.

The existence of hunter-killer teams remains to seek out and destroy those lives – and *only* those lives – deemed to be of irreparable harm to the nation deploying these units. Their function is not to take prisoners, nor to collect surveillance data and climatology reports. With the tenacity of a Gila monster, they exist to siphon evil out from the world one tyrannical individual at a time.

ABOUT THE AUTHOR

R.J. Godlewski (pronounced GOD LESS KEY) is the former executive manager of a threat resolution services business and served as the president of his own security company. He is an alumnus of American Military University, holding an M.A. in Military Studies, Asymmetrical Warfare concentration and a B.A. in Intelligence Studies, Terrorism Studies concentration (with minor degree in Area Studies, Middle East), both earned with academic honors. He further holds graduate and undergraduate certificates in Security Management and Explosive Ordnance Disposal, respectively. Mr. Godlewski is a veteran of both the U.S. Navy and U.S. Navy Reserve. He remains devoted to protecting the dignity and integrity of innocent human life, wherever and whenever it may be placed in jeopardy and by whatever means may be necessary and employs the breadth of his knowledge, experiences, and assets to achieve this mission.

His previous books include:

Practical Guerrilla Warfare

More Skills of the Assassin: Delving Deeper into Human Depravity

Skills of the Assassin: Understanding the Tactics of the Professional Killer

Fourth-Generation Corporate Security: Asymmetrical Warfare for Protective Services Professionals

Targeting Narco-Submarine Networks through Deep Penetration, Autonomous Maritime Irregular Warfare Units Operating within a Hunter-Killer Role